BRITAIN'S
FAVOURITE
ANIMALS

BRITAIN'S FAVOURITE ANIMALS

Contents

The lowlands have been farmed for centuries, creating a patchwork of arable land used for growing crops, and grassland for grazing cattle and sheep. Overgrown field boundaries and hedgerows provide refuges for wild animals that feed on the fields and pastures.

Britain is dotted with woodlands that act as havens for wildlife. Many have been heavily managed in the past, often by regular cutting or coppicing of hazel or chestnut to yield a renewable crop of young growth beneath the tall timber trees.

Introduction

The wild animals of Britain are mysterious creatures. They slip quietly through undergrowth and woodland, often by night, fearful of enemies and constantly sniffing the air for signs of danger. They may emerge into the open, but at the slightest alarm they melt away into cover. This makes every encounter with a truly wild animal a memorable experience. If you are upwind of the creature, so it has not detected your scent, and you have made no noise, suddenly it will be there – a fox, perhaps, trotting along a hedgerow, its beautiful russet coat glowing in the morning sun. Maybe a stoat will be caught offguard, gliding in and out of the cavities in a dry-stone wall in search of mice or small birds. You freeze, and marvel at the sight.

WHERE TO LOOK

Identity is rarely the issue – you know a fox when you see it – but if you want more than just a fleeting, tantalising, accidental glimpse,

▲ *A spring dawn on open grassland reveals the amazing sight of brown hares engaged in a 'boxing match' between a courting male and a reluctant female.*

you must know where and when to look, which means understanding how animals live and behave. *Britain's Favourite Animals* will give you the information that you need. You will discover what they eat, and when they are likely to be out and about. You will learn about their breeding habits, which in some species, such as the brown hare and red deer, involve spectacular displays performed in full view – if you are there to watch.

You will also find out whether these animals are likely to live near you. The animals in this book are arranged by their preferred habitats – farmland and grassland, woodland and coppice, moorland and upland, waterside and coast –

◄ *Although they have grown their beautiful adult coats, these young foxes are still too inexperienced to stray far from their den in a rocky outcrop.*

and in some cases, such as the mountain hare and water shrew, they are unlikely to be seen in any other type of landscape. However, many species – the wood mouse and hedgehog, for instance – range much more widely than their names suggest, turning up in all kinds of environments, including gardens and parks as well as woodland and field hedges.

Several animals, such as the pipistrelle and badger, are widespread throughout the British Isles, although many people never see them unless they take the trouble to go out at night and watch for them in the right places. Others, including the red squirrel and the pine marten, are restricted to just a few parts of Britain, yet they can still be seen if you know where to look. A few, such as the otter, are so shy and secretive that even seasoned wildlife watchers count themselves lucky to see one – yet the otter's very elusiveness makes it exciting, and a firm favourite with all animal lovers.

▲ *Cleaner waters and strict protection have helped the otter expand its range in recent years, both on wild rocky coasts and along many rivers.*

WILD REFUGES

Some of these animals are becoming increasingly rare. Water voles, for example, are far less common than they used to be, partly because of predation by introduced mink – also described in these pages – but mainly because of the loss of their wild habitats. All over Britain, wetlands have been drained and rough grassland ploughed up for growing crops. Brown hares are becoming scarce as farming has become more intensive, and dormice have suffered from the loss of ancient woodland.

Many animals have been forced to retreat to the few pockets of wilderness that remain. So when out in the countryside, or even urban commons and parkland, be aware of the needs of the animals that live there. Don't stray from the footpath, but stand or sit quietly and keep as still as you can. If you listen, watch and wait, you may find your patience is rewarded with the sight of an animal in its natural environment, and you will remember it forever.

▶ *This late-summer crop of sweet, energy-packed berries makes an ideal snack for a dormouse intent on building up its energy reserves before hibernation.*

CHAPTER 1 • FARMLAND AND GRASSLAND

The rabbit

An unmistakable sight on farmland and open grassland, these alert and inquisitive creatures are often deemed a nuisance because of their destructive feeding habits. Nevertheless, they are one of Britain's most popular animals.

Although it is so familiar that it seems like a native animal, the rabbit was in fact introduced to Britain from France by the Normans about 900 years ago. Originally, it was a major economic asset – a rapidly reproducing and conveniently sized source of fur and food arriving at a time when storage of meat from larger animals presented major problems.

Rabbits were kept in special walled enclosures called warrens – a term used today for any rabbit colony and its burrows. They were looked after by a warrener who fed them and provided protection from predators and poachers. Sometimes, rabbits had access to surrounding fields farmed by local peasants but returned to the warren for shelter.

Escapes were inevitable and rabbits became established on sandy heaths and clifftops where the soil was easy to dig and too poor for farming. As a result, nobody bothered to exterminate the escaped rabbits and their numbers steadily increased.

POPULATION EXPLOSION

In the 1700s, a major change in farming practice hugely benefited the rabbit. All over England, extensive hedgerows were created to enclose farmland. These provided rabbits with shelter from the weather and cover from predators, right alongside huge fields of food. They emerged from their burrows to fan out and devastate crops. Even today, corn planted near hedgerows is often eaten in spring, exposing bare soil, while farther out it is nibbled short.

Feral rabbits were often encouraged by the gentry, who valued them for hunting. At the same time, throughout the late 18th, 19th and early 20th centuries, rabbits benefited from landowners' and gamekeepers' ruthless persecution of predators that threatened other game, such as pheasants and grouse.

However, as a result of the damage they caused, most people considered rabbits to be a nuisance that could be harvested as part of the rural economy. So rabbits were trapped, snared and shot for their skins and meat. Professional rabbit catchers earned a living keeping numbers down on farms and around villages. Millions were killed annually, yet there seemed to be no decline in their numbers.

▶ The rabbit's eyes are very sensitive to movement and also highly effective in poor light conditions at night. However, they are unable to distinguish between different colours to any great extent.

BIOLOGICAL WARFARE

By the mid 20th century, rabbits had become Britain's most serious mammalian pest, doing more damage than rats and mice combined. Their depredations were estimated to cost over £50 million each year (more than £250 million today). In 1953, the myxoma virus was deliberately introduced to the rabbit population, and spread like wildfire. The virus was transmitted by rabbit fleas, and easily spread between individuals in confined burrows and underground nests. Blood-sucking mosquitoes carried it over wider distances.

The resulting disease, myxomatosis, was particularly nasty and almost always fatal. Within days, it caused swellings of the eyes and genital region. Soon the animal became blind. Unable to feed properly, an infected rabbit hopped around aimlessly, finally dying after about 11–15 days. In just two years, myxomatosis killed more than 99.99 per cent of the rabbit population. The devastation was so bad that numbers in some parts of Britain did not recover for 20 years. But while crops and wild plants were relieved of the effects of rabbit

▲ *Young rabbits come out to bask in the sunshine at the burrow entrance when they are about three weeks old. Rabbits are prolific breeders, producing up to seven or more in a litter. Despite threats from predators and illness, rabbit numbers remain high.*

damage, predators, such as buzzards, were deprived of an important source of food.

Today, myxomatosis is still present in the rabbit population, but the virus has weakened and rabbits seem to be less affected by it. Outbreaks now typically kill 40–60 per cent of

Rabbit radar

While hopping along, the rabbit picks up a sound that might mean danger. Rather than continuing to run, perhaps straight into trouble, it stops to find out more about the situation.

Turn tail and run!

The white flash of a rabbit's tail is very eye-catching. It acts as a warning to other rabbits, alerting them that some of their number are already running away from trouble.

infected animals, but rapid breeding easily makes up for such losses in a short time.

FAMILY LIFE

The rabbit is an exceptionally prolific animal. It starts to breed as early as January and may continue until August or even later. Females can produce up to seven or more young every five weeks or so throughout the summer. However, in high-density populations, breeding success is lower. Bad weather also reduces the rate of reproduction. Nevertheless, a single female may produce 20–30 offspring in a year – and these babies can breed at four months old, increasing the year's

total substantially. Small wonder that by late summer some areas may have as many as 40 or more rabbits per hectare (2½ acres).

Courtship involves much dashing about, with the male leaping past the female, often urinating on her at the same time. Mating is a very rapid process, taking only a few seconds. It takes place frequently and actually stimulates the female to ovulate, so rabbit sex results in conception more frequently than that of some other animals. When she is ready to give birth, a pregnant rabbit normally digs a short burrow, 1–2m (3–6½ft) long. This is called a 'stop' and has only one entrance and no side branches. Alternatively, she may use

a blind tunnel off one of the main burrows in a warren or, rarely, nest above ground. At the end of the stop, the mother-to-be makes a special nursery nest out of grass, moss or other plant material, and lines it with fur plucked from her own chest.

Female rabbit fur is normally well anchored to the skin, but the hormonal changes associated with pregnancy ensure that the fur of her chest and belly becomes looser and is easily pulled from the skin without discomfort. This fluffy bed will receive the young as they are born, and the mother crouches over her babies to suckle them. When she has to go to the surface, she carefully

◄ *Rabbits need to be constantly on the lookout for danger, since they are vulnerable to many predators. In long grass their view is obscured, so they often sit upright to check their surroundings. In short turf, they do not need to sit up so often.*

▶ *The act of mating is over in a flash. The male may briefly pass out and fall off the top of the female. Sometimes a pair stay together and mate several times, grooming each other in between. On other occasions, they simply go their own ways and continue feeding.*

seals the entrance of the burrow behind her to reduce the risk of predators finding her young. Many mother rabbits return just once each night to feed their offspring.

The young are pink and blind when they are born, covered in a faint wispy fur. Their eyes open at about 10 days and they begin to appear at the entrance to the stop at about three weeks of age. They are weaned, that is they can feed themselves, at about 25 days old, and may disperse. Those born later in the season may remain with their mother for much longer. During normal activity, rabbits rarely go more than 100m (about 300ft) from the safety of their burrow, but when they first become independent, young males may disperse up to 800m (½ mile) or more from where they were born. Females disperse less frequently and usually over smaller distances.

WARRENS AND TERRITORIES

The rabbit is a social species, living in small groups in a cluster of burrows. The dominant males rule the home and father most of the offspring. Females may fight fiercely to establish dominance among themselves, the winners gaining access to the best breeding sites. Adult females frequently attack their younger sisters, while the males may sometimes defend the youngsters.

Subordinate females are usually the youngest of the adults, born the same year and breeding for the first time. They will often have a shorter breeding season and be forced to make their stops away from the main burrow system, where their babies are more vulnerable to predators. The offspring of dominant females are more likely to become dominant themselves and command the best sites near the centre of the warren.

Each group of rabbits sets up a territory by running up and down the boundaries in full view of their neighbours to establish which group lives where. They define the territory with scent from their paws, creating shallow scrapes in the soil and leaving the scent as a marker. These scrapes are most numerous where rabbit territories meet. Strongly scented droppings are often deposited in clusters at the edge of the scrape or on top of a nearby ant mound or other prominent feature. Then the rabbits urinate on them, so the whole latrine is unmistakable.

SURVIVAL RATE

Large rabbit populations consume a lot of food and as autumn progresses and plant growth slows, many rabbits die from shortages. Over winter, population densities are usually between one and 15 per hectare (2½ acres), depending on food availability.

Although many babies are born in the spring and summer, the survival

Relaxed but ever watchful

Rabbits spend a lot of time curled up underground or hunched up feeding, and this can cause muscle fatigue and poor circulation. Just like tired humans, rabbits often stop what they are doing and stretch. But even though they may look relaxed, their ears are still busy scanning for the sound of predators.

rate is low. The average life expectancy of a newborn rabbit is about 11 weeks, and at least three-quarters usually die within the year. Sometimes up to 95 per cent of young animals will not survive to breed the following year.

There is also a marked difference in survival rates between young males and females. Males have to live a much more dangerous life than

females, going off to find new territory or, if they remain in the warren, patrolling the outer limits of existing territory, far from the safety of the burrows. Their lifestyle makes them vulnerable to attack by predators and as a result there are usually three females to every two males in the adult population.

Young rabbits are the preferred food of many predators, from buzzards to stoats and foxes or farm and feral cats, as well as weasels and badgers. Owls, great black-backed gulls and other birds will take rabbits, and many other species eat them as carrion. Road traffic kills many, especially at night when they are dazzled by headlights. Despite this, often more than half of the mature adults survive from one year to the next.

RABBIT FOOD

Rabbits like to live and feed in areas of short grass, close to their burrows – in fact they maintain this type of habitat by their feeding. They rarely

▲ *Rabbits not only nibble at crops and grass at ground level, they also rear up on their hind legs to reach the lower leaves of bushes and shrubs. This creates a 'browse line' in taller vegetation, just above rabbit head height.*

go far into long grass, partly because they do not like to eat coarse vegetation and partly because tall grass tends to be wet from rain or dew, causing the rabbit's fur to become soggy and matted. Also, in long vegetation they cannot see approaching predators, so they stay out in the open. Rabbits are particularly successful in lowland areas with well-drained soil, such as sand dunes and chalk downland. The soft fescue grasses that grow in these areas are a favourite food, and the terrain means their burrows remain dry, even in winter.

As well as soft grasses, they feed on horseshoe vetch, clover and crops. They will also gnaw the bark of trees, especially if snow covers their normal food supplies.

The harvest mouse

Often overlooked in summer among the tall grasses of field margins and reedbeds, the tiny harvest mouse is more easily seen when the vegetation dies down and it goes in search of winter quarters closer to the ground.

As its name implies, the harvest mouse has long been associated with ripe, golden cornfields. In the days when corn was cut by hand, these mice would be seen scampering out of the way during the harvest – the peak time for this smallest of European rodents as a result of numerous litters raised during the summer.

The Reverend Gilbert White, a renowned 18th-century naturalist, was the first to identify the species officially. He lived in Selborne in Hampshire and found the mouse living in cornfields around the village. Once people started to look for it, the mouse was found to be widespread throughout Britain. It is so tiny and unobtrusive, though, that it easily escapes notice and by the early 20th century, a lack of sightings led many naturalists to suggest it was dying out.

However, one reason it was rarely seen was that people were looking in the wrong places. The idea that cornfields were the main habitat of these creatures was a misconception. In fact, the harvest mouse has never established permanent populations in corn because the crop is removed every year. Each new crop needs to be re-invaded by mice from somewhere else. This 'somewhere else' is their permanent home and the best place to look for them.

▶ *Although the harvest mouse's vision is not particularly good, its bright eyes can detect movement and its acute hearing warns it of danger.*

A light and agile climber

Although traditionally associated with cereal crops, the harvest mouse lives and breeds in any tall grass. It is so tiny that it can climb swiftly and confidently among the slender stalks and flowers.

GRASSES AND REEDS

In summer, harvest mice are at home in tall grasses and weeds. They scramble about like miniature monkeys among the stems and leaves, building their summer nests off the ground. As well as cornfields they inhabit tussocks of sedges and grasses – cock's-foot is a favourite – hedge bases and marshland with tall vegetation. They will even live in reedbeds over standing water and in the long grass and bramble patches of wasteground.

POPULATION SURVEYS

In the early 1970s, conservationists organised surveys to look for harvest mice and the animal was quickly rediscovered, even in several parts of the Greater London area where it had previously been thought to be extinct. The Mammal Society carried out a national survey that confirmed harvest mice were common in many areas, including some places in Scotland and Wales where it had not been thought to live. The harvest mouse was not rare, as was feared – it had simply been overlooked.

When this survey was repeated 20 years later, in 1996–97, the picture was not so rosy. Field ecologists revisited over 800 of the places where harvest mice had been found in the 1970s to see if they were still there. Evidence of them was found in only about a quarter of the sites. The worst losses were in the cornfields of southern England, where more than 80 per cent of the former sites no longer had harvest mice present.

However, a number of more recent, localised surveys have produced conflicting results. Some suggest there has been a major decline over the last 30 years, others that the harvest mouse is actually far more common than previously thought. One such survey carried out in Essex, for example, found nests throughout the county, often about a kilometre (just over half a mile) away from previous sites. The harvest mice had merely moved to more suitable areas.

The decline recorded in the 1996–97 survey mirrors the growth in intensive farming and consequent destruction of habitat. However, the harvest mouse may be adapting and until another nationwide survey is carried out, searching for new places that the harvest mouse may have colonised, it is hard to be sure of its status. It may turn out to be under-recorded after all, especially taking into account annual population fluctuations.

CHANGING HABITAT

Hedges are ideal places for harvest mice to live, but many have been removed to make the bigger fields that are necessary to accommodate larger tractors and harvesters. Boggy areas with reeds and tall-stemmed plants, also ideal for harvest mice,

▲ *The agile harvest mouse can easily climb up thin stems to get to food that heavier animals cannot reach. It searches for insects, pollen and seeds among the flowers and stalks. However, extensive farming and intensive grazing of land have destroyed much of the harvest mouse's habitat.*

have been drained to provide more land for growing crops. Weedy field corners and edges have gone under the plough as a result of farming subsidies that encourage grain production. Weedkillers remove many plants that are good for harvest mice, while insecticides destroy an important part of their food. So, far from being an ideal habitat for harvest mice, cornfields have become one of the least likely areas where harvest mice can survive.

Away from arable fields, large areas of grazing land remain. However, most of this land is now grazed intensively, right to the edges, and not much tall, grassy vegetation survives. Any that remains is generally too short for harvest mice. Grassy fields that used to be grazed occasionally, or were perhaps mown for hay once a year, are now scarce. Previously such fields were common and harboured large numbers of harvest mice.

▶ *Grain forms a major part of the diet of the harvest mouse, but since the amount eaten is negligible, this rodent has never been persecuted by farmers. In fact, the mice help farmers by eating insects such as aphids.*

Much 'wasteland', often good for small rodents, has disappeared under housing estates and industrial developments, while road widening has destroyed many weedy verges. Others are regularly mown or treated with herbicide, again spoiling them for mice.

Despite all these hazards, there are grounds for optimism for the harvest mouse. Recent developments may well result in the restoration of suitable habitat. New protection for hedgerows, for instance, and various types of set-aside farming arrangements, whereby land is left fallow, should provide places for them to live, at least along the edges of fields. Another helpful factor is that less money is being allocated for land drainage.

It remains to be seen to what extent this tiny animal is able to recolonise lost ground. Harvest mice normally travel short distances only, and rarely move far from where they were born. Recolonisation may take a long time, unless aided by deliberate reintroductions. In some parts of Cheshire, this is already under way.

AVOIDING PREDATORS

In summer, harvest mice tend to spend much of their time up among the stalks of grasses and other plants, where it is difficult for predators to catch them. At the slightest threat, the mouse can leap to the ground and disappear into the thick grass, although where harvest mice become numerous, barn owls, major predators of all types of mice, may quickly learn to catch them and consume considerable numbers.

When the vegetation dies back during the autumn, harvest mice build winter nests low to the ground in grassy tussocks. They may also take up residence in the tunnels and

A useful tail

The harvest mouse has a prehensile tail. It can wrap the tip around thin objects to support its weight and can even hang by its tail, not needing any other support. This is especially useful when the animal is scrambling among stems of grasses that are swaying in the wind. Holding on by its tail steadies the mouse and reduces the risk of falling off. Getting a grip with its tail also allows the mouse to let go with its front paws, which it can then use like hands for other purposes, such as collecting food or gathering nest materials. When moving rapidly among grass stems, the tail is flicked from side to side to help maintain the mouse's balance.

Nest builders

The harvest mouse is the only British mammal to build its nest in tall grass, typically 30–60cm (1–2ft) above the ground. In tall reeds, nests may be sited higher still.

About the size of a tennis ball, the nest is woven from the shredded leaves of adjacent grasses. The mouse, sitting at the base of a leaf, pulls other leaves through its teeth to shred them. When enough are ready, it weaves them into a hollow ball, pulling more leaves inside through the walls of the nest. Once inside, these leaves are also shredded and incorporated into the structure while remaining attached to the grass stems outside.

Harvest mice particularly favour cock's-foot grass in which to nest. This forms tall tussocks and is used for about three-quarters of all harvest mouse nests. These nests, built up among tall stalks, are used in summer, larger ones for breeding and smaller, loosely woven ones – about 5cm (2in) in diameter – for sleeping in. Breeding nests are tightly woven and often lined with very finely chewed grass or even specially collected thistledown. Each litter has a new nest.

When the nests are first constructed, they are hard to spot because they are made of living grass and are green, just like all the surroundings. In autumn, when the grass withers, the nests become easier to see, but by then they are usually

empty because the mice have left for their winter quarters. In winter, harvest mice build small nests, low to the ground and deep within grass tussocks. These nests are more difficult to find. An artificial nest for a harvest mouse can be made out of an old tennis ball nailed some way up a stick, which is then pushed into the ground among tall grass. The entrance hole needs to be about 15mm (⅝in) in diameter. Harvest mice will set up home in them, just as birds use nestboxes.

burrows made by other small mammals. These provide shelter until new vegetation grows in spring and the mice can move back among the stalks. Harvest mice are particularly vulnerable in the autumn and winter, when there is little vegetation to provide cover, and they may seek refuge in barns and outhouses.

As well as owls, harvest mice are hunted by weasels and cats, but on the whole they are too small to interest many of the usual larger predators. Being so tiny, however, they are vulnerable to attack from unexpected quarters, such as crows, blackbirds and even toads.

SURVIVING THE WEATHER

The harvest mouse's size is a disadvantage in cold weather. Small animals find it more difficult to maintain their body temperature than larger ones and sharp frosts in the autumn reduce the population

substantially. Juveniles are especially vulnerable. Persistent rain batters down the tall grass stems, wrecking the harvest mouse's home, and heavy dew wets everything, threatening to clog the fur of these tiny creatures. This may cause them to lose body heat and die. Small wonder that most harvest mice do not live longer than six months.

YOUNG MICE

Harvest mice make up for such inevitable losses by prolific breeding. This begins in May and continues into the autumn, although about three-quarters of the young are born in August and September. Babies that are born in late autumn may be overtaken by bad weather and many die in the nest or soon after leaving home.

A litter consists of up to eight young although as many as 12 have been reported. Most of the adults

that have bred during the summer die soon afterwards, presumably because breeding is such a strain on them. Those that live longest are individuals that are born late in the year but escape bad weather, and do not breed until the following season. Some of these animals may live to be 18 months old, although this is very unusual. In captivity, safe from predators and severe weather, harvest mice have been known to live for five years.

The young weigh about 0.7g (a fraction of an ounce) at birth but grow extraordinarily fast. Fine, downy fur begins to grow on the fourth day and eyes open on the eighth or ninth day after birth. The babies begin to leave the nest and explore their surroundings when they are around 11 days old, and the mother abandons her family after they are weaned at around two weeks old. By this time, the female is often pregnant again. She then builds a new breeding nest nearby and raises another family.

A single female may have many families during the summer and early autumn. Some of the young will breed, which they can do at five weeks old, and their offspring may themselves be breeding before the summer is out. Populations can build up to high levels in the autumn, especially if cold weather is delayed until October or November, allowing time to raise yet more young. Many will die over winter, however, as the weather worsens and food supplies dwindle. Harvest mice do not hibernate but stay close the ground, where it is warmer.

CLOSE RANGE

Adults do not move around very much, having a home range of around 300 to 600 square metres (3200–6500sq ft), which is equivalent to a circle about 19–38m (60–125ft) in diameter. Ranges overlap, which indicates that

the species is not territorial, and in captivity they tolerate living very closely together.

In the spring, harvest mice may explore new areas in which to live. Even so, they rarely move more than 100m (330ft) or so from where they were born and prefer to travel along hedges and ditches, where the dense vegetation provides relative safety. As the grasses begin to grow tall, the young adults begin constructing new nests and the cycle starts over again.

▲ *Juicy berries form an important part of the harvest mouse's diet. The small insects the berries attract, such as fruit flies, are an additional, protein-rich source of food.*

▼ *In hedgerows and at the edge of wooded areas, a harvest mouse may come across new sources of food, such as fungi, as it clambers among the twigs and branches.*

The brown hare

Tawny-coloured fur ensures that the brown hare stands out in a snowy landscape as it sprints across open countryside. It takes fright at the faintest sound that might indicate a predator is in pursuit.

Unlike rabbits, brown hares do not use burrows or live in hedgerows. Instead, this distinctive mammal prefers open downs and farmland, and here it can be easily recognised. The best time to see the brown hare is in the early morning or late evening as it sits up on its hind legs to survey the scene. This is the time it usually ventures out to graze. The brown hare is mainly nocturnal but it may also be active during the day, especially if a good feeding ground has cover nearby. In winter, when

▼ *Powerful hind legs give the brown hare its momentum when running. Bringing them right forward either side of its front feet produces a strong drive.*

snow makes grazing difficult, the brown hare may be spotted during the day, tearing bark from saplings with its sharp teeth.

EQUIPPED FOR SURVIVAL

The brown hare's posture is generally alert. Located at the sides of the animal's head, its huge, unblinking eyes provide it with an all-round view of its surroundings. The brown hare also has a well-developed sense of smell and exceptionally sharp hearing. Its long, sensitive ears enable it to detect even slight sounds from afar that may be made by potential predators.

Renowned for its turn of speed, the brown hare's strong hind legs allow it to accelerate fast from a standing

start. When not being pursued, and so travelling in a more leisurely fashion, hares have a loping gait and cover the ground in long strides. When they run, they hold their tails down, so that the black tops are visible, unlike rabbits, which show the white undersides. Hares are usually silent but may emit a piercing scream if attacked or are otherwise in distress.

In winter, the brown hare's coat is thicker and a brighter russet than in the summer months, when it becomes lighter in density and colour. The brown hare moults in spring and autumn. To protect it from the harsh weather conditions of the open countryside, its body fur is dense with three different types of hairs –

the underfur, the pile hair and the top guard hairs. Individuals may be seen with unusual colour variations, including sandy coloured animals and albinos.

The brown hare's way of life seems perilous. It faces the dual challenges of being exposed to adverse weather and being easily spotted. Living in the open, with no burrows to hide in or woods to escape into, it is vulnerable to predators. These include foxes and large birds of prey, such as owls and buzzards, as well as humans, yet it is still able to survive in open countryside.

While the brown hare is mainly solitary in its habits, it is sociable at certain times. As well as getting together in pairs or groups during the breeding season, it may become more gregarious during foraging. Particularly in the evening, groups of brown hares may be seen feeding together. The presence of others provides each individual with the benefit of added security – it can spend more time feeding and less time watching out for predators. Even so, it is ever alert for danger and, even when feeding, does not keep its head down for long.

DAYTIME HIDEAWAY

The brown hare makes no nest, just a shallow depression of trampled or scraped out vegetation surrounded by long grass. This is called a form. There it crouches low and still to avoid detection and, unless disturbed, it re-uses the same form frequently. The brown hare lies with its hind quarters in the deepest part of the form and only its back and head visible. From a distance the animal is indistinguishable from a clod of earth. It may also retreat into

▶ *The hare's long, flexible body allows it to stretch tall to nibble at ripening maize. Although hares eat crops, they inflict less damage than rabbit colonies do.*

Speed and stamina

The brown hare relies for its survival on being able to out-distance its predators. Not only can the hare accelerate fast but it has the ability to keep running for a long time without slackening its pace.

woods and hedges to rest during the day, especially in windy weather. When giving birth, though, the hare stays out in the open, so its young have no nest or permanent home.

CHARACTERISTIC SIGNS

A few clues may indicate the presence of hares. Gaps made in hedges or fences, for instance, where the animals have pushed their way through. They may also leave trails of flattened grass across farmland.

Hare droppings cannot always be reliably distinguished from those of rabbits because their character is dependent on what the hares have been eating. However, they are usually larger, lighter in colour and more fibrous than rabbit droppings.

When it comes to tracks, both rabbits and hares have four toes on each foot, but hares' paws are larger. The tracks can be distinguished from those of larger animals, such as dogs, because the furry soles of hares' paws often blur the outline of the pads.

FARMLAND FEEDING

Brown hares are patchily dispersed around Britain, which may in part be due to the farming year. The brown hare normally stays in a general area of 20–40 hectares (50–100 acres), but moves about seasonally as food availability changes. Prior to the introduction of modern farming practices, farmers tended to grow a variety of crops so that brown hares could move from, for example, turnip tops to grass or cereals simply by travelling around one farmstead.

Feeding on arable land has become more challenging for the hare because farmers now tend to specialise, growing just one or two crops on their land. Once a crop has been harvested and the earth ploughed, there is little to eat in that location until the next crop has had time to grow. Large areas of countryside may provide no food for brown hares for many weeks, and so they have to travel farther afield to feed, possibly two kilometres (just over a mile) per day.

SHARING PASTURE

Livestock farms present brown hares with a different set of problems. On permanent pastures, farmers tend to keep as many cattle or sheep as possible and the animals' presence is disturbing and distracting for hares. They have to remain constantly alert and often have to move from their

◄ *Even in infancy, hares are solitary animals. After suckling from their mother the leverets scatter immediately, each returning to its form.*

Mad March hares

In late winter and spring, the mainly solitary brown hare may be seen in pairs or in small courtship groups. The expression 'mad as a March hare' derives from its behaviour during the breeding season. From about late January, males attempt to stay close to females that are ready to breed, but frequently have to leave them to chase away rivals.

Courtship involves 'boxing' as the female rears up on hind legs, thrashing and pawing at the male, who tries to defend himself. This feverish activity is most likely to be seen in the middle of the breeding season – in March – hence the reference to March madness, but the breeding season of brown hares continues throughout the summer. Later, crops and long grass make hares much less conspicuous, creating the impression that this behaviour occurs only in March.

forms as a cow or sheep wanders too close. Hares are not only less able to feed effectively or rest properly during the day, but have to compete with the farm animals for food.

GRASSLAND DANGERS

On some farms, grasslands may be ploughed up and re-seeded each year to grow high-quality grass for silage. The grass is ripe for cutting and carting away at the peak of the hare's breeding season. Instinctively, hares and leverets crouch motionless in their forms to wait for the noisy farm vehicles to pass by. Many are run over and killed. Today's farm machines are so fast and powerful that there is little opportunity for the hares to escape even if they do realise the imminent danger.

The use of herbicides and pesticides, as well as reducing the hare's food, presents another threat. The chemicals are usually lethal if they are accidentally sprayed on to hares, or if they get into a hare's fur as the animal pushes through a sprayed hedgerow and are swallowed during grooming.

HUMANS AND HARES

Hares may cause losses to crops and damage growing trees, so farmers and landowners do not welcome excessive numbers. Until recently, hares were hunted by humans using packs of beagles that followed the animals by scent. In coursing, fast dogs were let loose to chase the hares, which had often been caught previously in nets for release. Such practices are now banned in Britain, although organised winter hare shoots do still occur.

Despite their decline in numbers – around 75 per cent over the last 50 years – the law offers brown hares little protection, although the Hares Preservation Act of 1892 prohibits the sale of hares and leverets from March to July. At this time, British hares must not feature on restaurant menus.

Courtship antics

Brown hares do not live in colonies as rabbits do but nevertheless, early in the year, they congregate for the onset of the breeding season. At this time brown hares – particularly males – are highly excitable.

The hedgehog

For most of the year Britain's only spiny mammal forages for food each night, searching through grassy fields and hedgerows. In winter, however, it curls up to sleep among dead leaves and other vegetation.

Despite its secretive and largely nocturnal habits, the hedgehog is one of Britain's best-loved creatures. Its spiny coat makes it unmistakable. A frequent visitor to suburban gardens, the hedgehog often benefits from food put out by well-disposed wildlife watchers. In return, they get an intriguing glimpse of their visitor when it appears each evening to snuffle and snort at the food bowl. But despite their familiarity, few people ever get the chance to inspect a hedgehog closely – it is a timid creature when humans approach,

and capable of unexpected turns of speed. The hedgehog's thousands of spines also make it hard to examine the details of its body, and if caught or threatened, the hedgehog rolls into a tight ball, showing few of its more vulnerable parts.

The spines are modified hairs that become sharp and rigid as the hedgehog matures. They cover the animal's back and sides, while the belly is covered by long sparse hair that offers little insulation or protection. This hair is probably better suited to the hedgehog's low-level lifestyle than soft fine fur, which

would become wet and matted as it trundled around in wet grass.

Surprisingly, hedgehogs can run quite fast – at up to about 10 kilometres per hour (6mph), even more over short distances. The feet have five toes, each of which is furnished with a long, but not very sharp, claw, used mainly for scraping away soil and leaves in search of

▼ *Families normally consist of mother plus four or five babies, but sometimes there may be as many as seven. They stay together for about six weeks, before dispersing to live on their own.*

Myth and folklore

Hedgehogs are reputed to attack and eat snakes, and have indeed occasionally been seen eating adders. But it is unlikely that hedgehogs are the aggressors – in reality the snake may end up with self-inflicted wounds from attacking such a well-armoured target, leaving the hedgehog simply to finish it off.

Other tales suggest that hedgehogs suckle milk from cows, even though they are too short to reach the udder. If a cow is lying down, however, milk often seeps from the teats and could conceivably attract a passing hedgehog to latch on. They might even come specially as hedgehogs are very fond of milk and may be attracted by its smell. However, cow's milk can upset a hedgehog's digestion. For this reason, hedgehogs should never be given large amounts of milk in the garden – in the wild, if a hedgehog did manage to find some cow's milk, the effect would be diluted by other elements of its diet. Another widespread folk tale is that hedgehogs collect fallen apples on their spines by rolling on them and then carrying the fruit off to their nests. Although hedgehogs will eat squashy fruits, and occasionally one may have accidentally impaled its spines on a fallen apple, this story is hard to believe. Food is not normally carried away, nor is it stored in the nest. Nevertheless, the story has persisted for centuries and turns up in the folklore of many different countries.

food. The hedgehog's tail is about 2cm (¾in) long, but is normally hidden by its overhanging spiny coat.

Altogether, the hedgehog is well-adapted to sifting through dead leaves and other ground cover in search of invertebrate prey. Few people realise that hedgehogs are one of the most ancient types of mammal alive today. They evolved over 15 million years ago, and have survived, essentially unchanged, through geological changes, ice ages and the rise of Man, while more spectacular species have flourished briefly and become extinct.

SENSES AND SALIVATION

Although its ears are not especially large, the hedgehog relies on them a great deal. On hearing a sudden noise, it freezes and bristles its spines. Being close to the ground, it can hear its prey – even worms and beetles sound quite noisy to sensitive ears so low down.

Smell is also important – the snout has a large moist tip, and the parts of the brain used to interpret scents are well developed, an indication of how useful this sense is to hedgehogs. They use smell to find food and can easily follow scent trails, so they probably use smell to detect and recognise each other as well.

Sight is less vital, as down in the undergrowth they cannot see very far anyway – even blind hedgehogs can survive quite well. Indeed, hedgehogs' night vision is probably no better than that of some humans.

One very unusual aspect of hedgehog behaviour is known as self-anointing. Sometimes after chewing a sharp-tasting or strong-smelling substance, but often with no apparent trigger, a hedgehog will start to produce copious amounts of frothy saliva. It then twists and turns frenetically to spread the foam all over its body using its tongue. This can go on for an hour or more, with the animal completely engrossed in this seemingly bizarre activity. Self-anointing occurs in both sexes and in young as well as adults. Nobody knows why hedgehogs do it, and no other animal behaves in this way.

ON THE SCROUNGE

Hedgehogs find their food by foraging, and they can often travel as much as 2–3km (1–2 miles) each night. Males are especially active and, in the breeding season, some may clock up 4km (2½ miles) before returning to their nest at dawn. A different nest may be used each day or two, especially in summer, with

Natural blond

Hedgehog spines are usually banded in brown and cream, giving the animal a grizzled appearance. However, in some animals the dark pigments fail to develop, leaving the spines a pale cream or white. These are not real albinos, but 'blond' hedgehogs. They are very rare in mainland Britain, but on Alderney, in the Channel Islands, a quarter of all the hedgehogs are this attractive colour. This probably results from inbreeding among the small number of animals that were originally released there.

sites scattered over a wide area. By contrast, females often have a much smaller range, using the same nest every day for a couple of weeks before moving on. Different hedgehogs may use the same nest.

Although hedgehogs are usually active only after dark, around midsummer, when nights are short, they may come out early and still be active after dawn. At night, they are more likely to find their favourite foods, including caterpillars, slugs, worms and beetles. The hedgehog's front teeth point forward, making a scoop to seize small prey, such as

spiders. Curiously, the lower front teeth bite into a gap between the upper ones. This reduces the power of the grip, so hedgehogs cannot deliver much of a bite and rarely manage to draw blood from humans or large animals. The teeth are quite blunt, especially in older animals that have eaten a lot of gritty earthworms.

As well as invertebrates, hedgehogs also eat carrion, including dead mammals and birds. Occasionally they will even attack live mice and the chicks of ground-nesting game birds. This habit, combined with a predilection for birds' eggs, makes

them unpopular with gamekeepers, who kill several thousand hedgehogs each year as a consequence. Predation on eggs and chicks is now recognised to have had a serious effect on seabird and wader populations where hedgehogs have been introduced close to nest sites on islands naturally free of such predators.

COAT OF SPINES

One of the main reasons for the hedgehog's success is its most distinctive characteristic – its spines, which bristle aggressively when the animal is threatened or attacked.

Midnight feast

Out on patrol, the hedgehog is constantly sniffing out tasty morsels to eat. Almost any small living thing at ground level will be investigated and, in many cases, eaten. Hedgehogs are quite noisy eaters and sometimes may be heard even when they cannot be seen.

Rolled up and encased in its spiny skin, the hedgehog is so well protected that few predators will touch it, although foxes, polecats, owls and eagles may take the occasional one. Very young babies are vulnerable because their spines are not fully developed and they are not yet able to roll up properly. Generally, however, hedgehogs have little to fear except badgers and cars. Badgers kill quite a few hedgehogs and, as their populations increase, it is possible that hedgehog numbers will decline in some places.

Road traffic kills many more hedgehogs than any natural enemy. Nobody knows how many die on the roads each year, but it may be as many as 100,000.

▲ *Hedgehogs can swim, but sadly often drown in even quite small ponds because the smooth sides of plastic pond liners offer no chance of escape. An escape ramp or some chicken wire dangling into the water allows the animals to climb out of a pond before they tire and drown.*

Hedgehogs are also at risk from careless gardeners, falling victim to lawnmowers and bonfires or succumbing to pesticides scattered on the garden or accumulated in slugs and other prey. As their habitat becomes more developed, hedgehogs increasingly meet their end in swimming pools and on building sites.

Provided they avoid all these hazards, hedgehogs can live for up to seven years, and exceptionally to ten. However, the majority probably survive for about three years and many die young. Females are able to breed in the year following their own birth, and usually produce about four young in a litter. These are usually born in June and July, but there are some late births in September or even October. Late-born young will be lucky to survive if cold weather comes early.

HIBERNATION HABITS

The hedgehog is one of Britain's few true hibernators. Its body shuts down for the winter to save energy while food is in short supply. Apart from a few brief periods of wakefulness, it usually sleeps from November to March, although younger hedgehogs may still be active as late as Christmas, especially in mild weather, as they try to fatten up as much as possible.

Winter is spent in a nest made of leaves. The hedgehog gathers them in small bundles in its mouth and pushes them into a heap below a

◀ *Thousands of spines make up the hedgehog's coat and keep it safe from most threats. Its mottled colouring also acts as good camouflage.*

▶ *The hedgehog's attention is normally concentrated on the ground immediately in front of its nose as it seeks out food. The head is raised periodically to sniff the air and listen for more distant movements.*

bush or garden shed. Then it burrows inside and shuffles about to arrange the leaves as a thick covering all round its body. Young hedgehogs are inexperienced at making nests, and often need several attempts – it is important to get it right as the nest is the hibernating animal's only protection from cold and bad weather, and must remain intact and waterproof for at least five months.

The availability of suitable nest-building materials is vital, and this is probably why hedgehogs are rarely found in places where naturally fallen leaves are scarce, such as moorland and dense pine woods. For the same reason, hedgehogs suffer when leaves are cleared away and suitable nest sites in towns and gardens are tidied up.

POPULATION CHANGES

There are probably between one and two million hedgehogs in Britain, but researchers have no really accurate way to estimate their numbers. Moreover, they do not know for certain if the species is holding its

own or declining. Hedgehogs are still widespread and fairly common, yet the majority of experts suspect they are less numerous than they were.

This possible decline in the hedgehog population is chiefly due to loss of habitat. A century ago, the British landscape was dotted with paddocks and small fields bounded by hedgerows. Short grazed turf with nearby dense cover was ideal for the hedgehog. Today, intensive farming means that much of this habitat has been replaced by arable crops, and hedgerows have been removed in order to provide access for large agricultural machines. The new landscape offers far less hedgehog food and fewer refuges.

Many find useful retreats in towns and gardens, but these are often too small and too tidy to provide food and nest sites. Urban developments leave hedgehogs isolated in small pockets that cannot be renewed from outside. However, thanks to humans, hedgehogs that do survive in urban areas often find more food than in many parts of the countryside.

The mole

Easily located thanks to the mounds of earth it leaves on open grassland, the ever-active mole burrows night and day to excavate an often extensive network of underground tunnels in which to trap its prey.

Most people are familiar with the work of moles from seeing the characteristic heaps of soil that they throw to the surface as they dig their underground tunnels. Molehills are among the most distinctive sights on British grasslands and grassy spaces, and are so easy to recognise that the mole's distribution is better known than that of any other native mammal – it is found almost everywhere except Ireland and some smaller islands.

Yet despite the familiarity of molehills, few people have ever seen one of the animals themselves. This is because moles spend nearly all of their time underground and out of sight in a damp, dark environment. Here, they burrow through the earth, unseen and undetected, until they eject a pile of soil above ground, often to the fury of the lawn-lover and gardener.

BORN TO BURROW

The mole is a squat creature, supremely adapted to its burrowing lifestyle. It has short, usually dark fur, a cylindrical body and a tapering head that appears to join directly to the body without a neck. Broad front paws stick out from the front of the body, with no apparent sign of arms. This unusual design has evolved to ensure that moles can

exert very powerful leverage with their forelimbs. The upper arm bone is short, almost rectangular and hidden from sight within the creature's fur. This shape creates a relatively enormous area for the attachment of digging muscles, and makes the mole amazingly strong for its size. Anyone who picks up a live mole is immediately astonished by how powerful this small animal is. Moles are easily able to burst a firm human grip, forcing the fingers apart as though thrusting aside heavy soil.

In contrast, the mole's hind legs are slender and are used to propel the animal along its tunnels. They are also jammed into the burrow wall for stability while the mole uses its front feet to dig, and to kick the earth backwards out of the way during tunnelling. As the mole's limbs are so well adapted for other tasks, they are rarely used to support its body. Instead, its weight rests on its belly, and the mole has thick, tough skin on its underside to cope with this – in most mammals the skin on the stomach is usually the thinnest.

▶ *Powerful legs allow a mole to bury itself completely within a few seconds. In loose soil, the mole almost 'swims' into the ground.*

▶ *When a mole catches an earthworm, it pulls the animal between its hands to scrape off most of the gritty soil stuck to the worm's surface. This action also squeezes unwanted soil out of the worm's intestine.*

TELLING TAILS

At the end of its body, the mole has a small tail, about 2cm (¾in) long. Despite its size, the tail is very important to the mole's underground lifestyle. It is carried pointing upwards, like a flagpole, constantly feeling the way along tunnels. This is especially useful when the mole needs to travel backwards – although the mole can twist itself around within the tight confines of its burrow, it usually finds it easier to reverse. Stiff tail hairs are linked to sense organs in the tail itself, allowing the mole to identify and interpret obstacles in its path. The tail is so effective that moles can run backwards almost as fast as they can move forwards.

To assist in reversing, its fur is also specially adapted. Any other mammal would be slowed down by the lie of its fur, which normally points backwards and would be forced in the wrong direction by tight-fitting burrow walls, jamming the animal in the tunnel. A mole's coat has hairs that can lie either forwards or backwards with equal ease. This, and the very fine, silky texture of the hairs, gives the fur a velvety feel, and it was once much prized for use in waistcoats and coat collars.

MULTICOLOURED MOLES

Mole fur is longer in winter than in summer, growing to 9mm (⅜in) as opposed to 6mm (¼in). Unusually, the hairs are of almost uniform length over the whole body – most mammals have longer hair on some parts of the body than on others. The fur is almost always black, but ash-grey varieties occasionally occur, as do orange, cream and piebald ones. White moles include true

All in a day's work

Moles can be active both by day and night. A typical day consists of three periods of activity – spent digging, feeding and patrolling their network of tunnels – and in between, the animal returns to its nest to rest and sleep.

Curiously, moles usually start work at the same time each day, regardless of the season, even though they can have little knowledge of whether it is day or night outside their underground burrow.

Perhaps enough light filters down through loose soil to provide clues, or maybe the activity of birds and other animals above can be heard by the mole.

Males are generally more active than females, and in the breeding season they may stay away from their nest for several days at a time, sleeping in odd corners of their seasonally enlarged burrow system.

albinos. These colour varieties appear in about 1 per cent of the population, which makes them extremely common compared to variations in other small mammals. One explanation may be that even pale moles are relatively safe from predators because they are underground. By contrast, a very pale mouse would be quickly seen and eaten by an owl or other predator, so its peculiar colour could not be passed on to the next generation. Moles can survive whatever their colour, so perhaps the surprise is that so many are simply black.

SIGHT, SOUND AND SCENT

At first glance, a mole's head appears to be completely lacking ears and eyes, and folklore often has it that moles are blind. In fact, both sets of sensory organs are present, but apparent only on close examination. The ears are about 5mm (¼in) long and hidden in the mole's fur. The eyes are the size of pin heads and are normally closed. A mole's sight is not as good as our's, but it can see movement and tell light from dark, although it cannot distinguish colours. Large eyes would fill with earth during digging, so the mole has evolved to live with tiny ones.

Dropping in for dinner

The earthworms, insects and centipedes that fall through the roof of the mole's tunnel try to dig their way back out, so potential prey is continuously entering and leaving the burrow. The mole moves through its tunnels, catching and eating as many of its unwitting guests as possible.

To compensate for its poor eyesight, the mole has a highly developed sense of smell – its most important sense apart from touch, and the one it mostly uses in hunting its invertebrate prey. The mole's snout ends in a flat plate, like a pig's nose. This area of bare pink skin is incredibly sensitive to touch. Pimple-like growths called Eimer's organs cover the surface and detect tiny movements, as well as changes in temperature and humidity.

Scent is enormously important to moles as a means of communicating with each other, since their vision is almost useless underground. They leave scent marks on the walls of the tunnels, which are renewed every time the animal brushes by. These pungent signs act as a warning to others to stay away and appear

Busy life

The mole is a very active creature both above and below the surface. It scurries about, pushing its sensitive nose into any place that might harbour food.

to be very effective, as moles are almost never found occupying each other's tunnels.

BREEDING

It is very difficult to tell mole sexes apart because they are so well protected by fur and there is very little external difference between males and females. Moles distinguish each other by scent. Their belly fur is often discoloured by brownish yellow secretions from scent glands, called preputial glands, that are located beneath the skin. These secretions are particularly noticeable during the breeding season.

Moles live solitary lives. They belligerently expel intruders, except for just a few hours each year when the female is on heat. During this period a receptive female mole will tolerate the presence of a male, and leaves a scent message to indicate to a potential mate that it is safe to approach her.

Moles can breed when they are one year old. The female gives birth to three or four young, occasionally more, usually around April or May

▼ *Moles spend most of their time underground, but they surface to catch food and collect nest material, and when they move from the tunnel where they were born to dig a burrow of their own. It is at this time that they fall prey to owls and other predators.*

(later in Scotland). The young are tiny, naked, and blind at birth. Their fur begins to grow at two weeks old and they start to leave the nest and become independent between 35 and 40 days after birth. Juvenile moles leave their mother's tunnel system as soon as they are weaned, otherwise she will drive them away. Moles will not tolerate lodgers competing for food, even their own offspring. The numbers born seem to be just enough to maintain the population. Unlike the populations of many small mammals, which vary greatly from year to year, mole numbers appear to be remarkably stable.

LEAVING HOME

Young moles must find an unoccupied area in which to set up home. This is not easy, especially where population densities are high. Young moles can travel farther and faster on the surface than by burrowing, but this can be dangerous. Some probably make quite long journeys, and may cross inhospitable ground. They mostly travel in darkness, but are then vulnerable to attack by owls and other predators, including badgers, foxes, cats and dogs. Tawny owls take a high proportion of moles in early summer, when many juveniles are moving from their maternal homes. Many other young moles are the victims of cars.

TUNNEL VISION

It is a popular misconception that moles dig through the soil to catch worms. This would be totally impractical because the mole would expend far more energy moving soil than it would recoup eating the prey it came across. In fact, the mole excavates a series of burrows that form a permanent tunnel system. This serves as a giant pit trap for any worms, beetles and other invertebrates that happen to be wriggling their way through the

soil. If they break into the mole's tunnel, they will be exposed and vulnerable to attack. The mole constantly patrols its tunnels on the lookout for such creatures.

Where large numbers of prey animals are present, the mole can survive with a relatively small burrow system and high densities of moles can occur. Conversely, in poor sandy soils, worms and other soil animals are less frequent, so each mole needs a larger tunnel system. The number of moles per hectare is consequently lower in such places. The number of molehills is never a true indication of the size of a population. Sandy soils are light and easy to dig, and extending the tunnel system and creating more molehills is not difficult. Accordingly, some

▲ *Moles are supremely adapted to tunnelling underground, but are not much good at moving about on the surface. They propel themselves in a rather ungainly way, with their hands held vertically because they are unable to place them flat on the ground.*

sandy areas have huge numbers of molehills, caused by maybe just two or three moles.

Although moles spend most of their lives in their burrows, it is wrong to imagine that they are never active at the surface. As well as the need to disperse, shortage of food may also drive them above ground. This happens commonly during hot dry summers, when a long period of drought will cause earthworms to burrow deep in the soil and become inactive. The mole's normal supply of worms dwindles dangerously and finding food can be very difficult. Faced with this problem, many moles will emerge at night or around dawn to seek other food in the dew-dampened grass.

CLOSE PROXIMITY

Moles occur in a variety of habitats, even where there is only a thin layer of soil on top of solid rock. They are common in deciduous woodland, though their presence often goes unnoticed because the molehills are hidden by fallen leaves. Here, they may live at a density of four or five per hectare (2½ acres). They are more obvious in farmland, especially pasture, where the habitat is rich in food. There may be up to 16 moles living in a hectare of good pastureland in the summer months. They also invade arable fields, where the molehills are obvious soon after ploughing, but are soon obscured by the growing crops.

Deep ploughing and heavy rolling of the soil make life difficult for moles. They are often driven out of crop fields and have to recolonise from nearby woods and hedgerows, moving into parks and gardens. Similarly, winter floods can force moles to retreat from low-lying areas – but they usually return, lines

of their molehills spreading outwards from hedge banks and higher ground. Moles can also be found in upland areas, but tend to be scarcer at high altitudes. This is partly because the soil is difficult to tunnel but also because worms and other prey are in shorter supply. Moles are infrequent in conifer plantations and heathlands for similar reasons.

▲ *Excavated soil has to be ejected after every few metres of tunnelling. The resulting molehills are not burrow entrances, but do indicate the mole's route underground.*

Disappearing act

Moles are very vulnerable on the surface and remain exposed for as short a time as possible. If a mole is surprised, it will scrabble vigorously with its hind feet in order to get back down into its burrow system as fast as it can.

The field vole

Leaving the safety of its burrow to feed is risky for the field vole. Scampering along the well-worn runways it makes in long grass, it is concealed from predatory birds but still vulnerable to attack from foxes and badgers.

This small mammal plays a crucial part in the natural foodchain. Few of Britain's predators could maintain their present populations without the field vole. Wildcats, pine martens and weasels all depend heavily on this species for food, as do many predatory birds, such as barn owls. They are also a useful addition to the diets of kestrels, badgers and even eagles and herons. Foxes seem to prefer field voles to all other small mammals.

Field voles' preferred habitat is long, tussocky grass and they are rarely found anywhere else. They eat grass, make nests of it and burrow among its roots and stems. Few other species of British mammals are so restricted in their habitat, yet because permanent grassland is so widespread in Britain, especially in the uplands, there is plenty of space for these animals to survive in very large numbers. Despite this, numbers are declining, although the field vole may still be Britain's most numerous wild mammal, with a total population of around 75 million before the start of the breeding season.

GRASS KINGDOM

Lack of grazing on grassland allows scrub and woody vegetation to spread. Without sufficient grazing activity the woody scrub becomes so dense that it shades the grass from the sun, causing it to wither. In turn, field voles suffer as their food declines and their grassy world begins to disappear.

On the other hand, if there is too much grazing – or mowing – the grass becomes too short to provide cover, and sooner or later they are eaten by predators. This is exactly what has happened in many farmland and suburban areas, where livestock and mowing machines create a short-grass habitat unsuitable for voles.

POCKETS OF ABUNDANCE

Once the field voles have gone from an area they are unlikely to return, because they do not travel very far, especially over open farmland or across wide roads. Therefore, despite their abundance nationally, field voles are now absent or scarce in many parts of the lowlands, leading to extremely patchy populations. Even in the uplands, sheep can graze grass right down while planting conifer plantations destroys the habitat on which the voles depend.

▶ *Although the field vole feeds mainly on the succulent lower stems of grasses, it may venture out from a field edge to sample an arable – especially a cereal – crop.*

◄ A nest may be exposed when grassland is cut, but if it is quickly covered up again, the female field vole will probably not desert her young.

FOOD FOR THOUGHT

All this bodes ill for field voles, which is also bad for their predators. Although other species of small mammals may move in to take the place of field voles as the habitat changes, they are often harder to catch. Wood mice, for example, are happy to live in short grass, but are very fast on their feet and easily evade predators. Bank voles move in with scrub encroachment but again are a poor substitute for their grass-loving cousin because the scrub makes it harder for owls and mammalian predators to get at them. Catching field voles in open grassland is easy by comparison.

Predators that are forced to rely on species of small mammals other than the field vole for food soon find themselves spending far more energy in capturing their prey, but obtaining only the same amount of food for their trouble. An adult barn owl, for instance, might manage to sustain itself on bank voles or wood mice, but be unable to catch enough of these rodents to raise a family. This is why any efforts to conserve the barn owl, or reintroduce pine martens, must first concentrate on

Field vole numbers have declined over the last 50 to 100 years as a result of increasingly efficient farming, which has found ways to utilise previously uncultivated land. In lowland areas, 'wasteland', which is ideal for field voles, has been eagerly snapped up by developers to build roads, houses, out-of-town supermarkets and to cater for activities that leave little room for the long grass that the voles need.

Rabbits have also caused problems, because they nibble grassland into very short, trimmed 'lawns'. Rabbit numbers have steadily increased since the disastrous affects of myxomatosis in the 1950s, and where they have become more numerous, the field vole has been in retreat.

Island home

Field voles are absent from Orkney, but a race of the European common vole, the Orkney vole (*Microtus arvalis orcadensis*), lives there. This may have been introduced by Stone Age settlers some 5400 years ago. Orkney voles probably originated from southern Europe. They were once abundant, but intensive use of farmland means that today the voles are restricted to grassy strips alongside ditches and roads and in the less suitable habitats of moorlands and bogs. The total population probably consists of fewer than one million animals.

Orkney voles build tunnels in the grass and are active during the day and night at about three-hour intervals. They usually return to a grassy nest to sleep, but may take short naps in their tunnels. They eat grass and other vegetation. The voles breed throughout the summer, producing relatively small litters. Nevertheless, high densities of animals may build up, over 250 per hectare (2½ acres) in good habitats. The young breed the year after their birth and die soon afterwards. A different race of the European common vole is found on Guernsey.

the condition of local habitats in terms of supporting a thriving field vole population.

The many field voles that are taken by predators are soon replaced because voles are prolific breeders. The females usually produce their first young by late March or early April and continue to breed until October. They have a succession of litters (between two and seven), one after the other, throughout the summer – sometimes even during the winter. Each litter typically comprises about four to six babies, which take just two weeks to rear. The young female voles are themselves able to breed at four weeks of age, while the

▼ *Emerging from its grassland burrow, this field vole is taking a great risk by moving out into the open to investigate possible food. If it remains here for long, it may be snatched up by a hunting bird such as a kestrel.*

males take a further two weeks to reach maturity. This means that voles born early in the season can themselves soon be breeding, contributing yet more babies to the population.

RISE AND FALL

Field vole populations follow a boom and bust pattern. In some years, at about three to five-year intervals, vole numbers can build up to very high levels, followed by a population crash. These booms often occur where long grass is available in a suitable place, such as in areas that have been fenced off to plant conifers. Fencing keeps out sheep, allowing the grass to grow long and thick. Here the voles flourish, at least for a few years until their grassy habitat is succeeded by the trees, which shade out the grass and the voles have to go elsewhere. Moorland

vole predators, such as hen harriers and short-eared owls, prosper during this period.

Outside conifer plantations, predators generally help to suppress the field vole's cycles of abundance. In good vole years, owls and birds of prey benefit and often manage to rear more young themselves. Where there are insufficient predators, however, vole numbers reach plague proportions and the animals may inflict considerable damage on the vegetation. During the 1890s and again in the 1920s and 1930s there were many instances of 'vole plagues', where field voles became so numerous that they caused significant damage to farm crops and newly planted trees. Where the animals had been forced out of their preferred habitat by sheer pressure of numbers, they invaded other habitats and even damaged orchard fruit trees by gnawing at the bark.

Bright eyes and twitching nose

In the mysterious hours of twilight, a field vole emerges from its nest and scurries along the network of runways it has worn through the long grass. It sprays the path with a pungent scent as it goes.

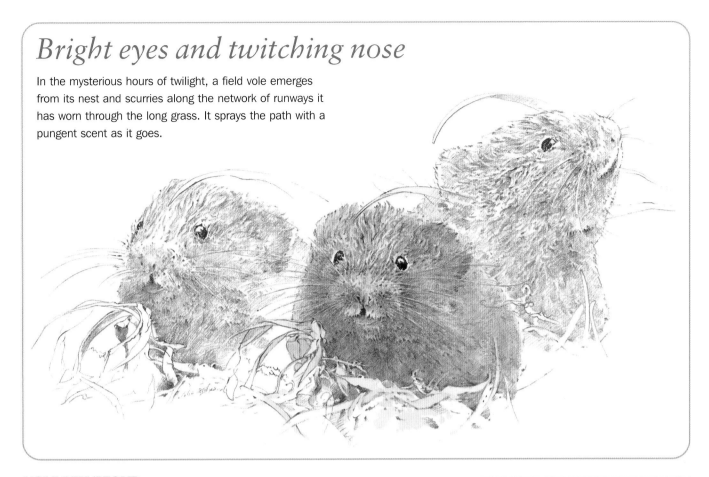

VOLE BEHAVIOUR

Field voles are aggressive little creatures, especially the adult males, which defend exclusive territories against rivals. Adult females fiercely defend their nests and young. However, they are tolerant of their own offspring and juvenile females often manage to remain within their mother's territory or close by. Young males are driven out, probably by their father, and so have to find somewhere new to live. This helps to prevent the population from becoming locally inbred.

Field voles do not disperse very far, rarely travelling beyond a few hundred metres from their nest, nor do they live very long. Probably fewer than 5 per cent of field voles live to be more than about 18 months old and very few survive through a second winter.

Field voles are active at all times of the day, although in summer they are mainly nocturnal, with peaks of activity around dawn and dusk. In winter, very cold nights encourage them to emerge during the day. They are often busier on wet days, too, perhaps because the creatures that hunt them prefer to avoid the rain.

SCENT SIGNALS

Field voles scurry about in their tunnels, keeping in touch with each other by leaving scent markers via large sensory glands on their hips. The smell is deposited with urine and piles of droppings, and other voles passing by can 'read' these signs and interpret the smells to determine who is in the vicinity.

Experiments have shown that individual voles can recognise their own species by smell, and it is likely that they can also tell the sex and breeding condition of other voles. Field voles are also quite vocal, especially during aggressive encounters. However, these noises are exactly what an owl or fox may be waiting to hear before pouncing to secure a meal.

Ears and teeth

Given its close association with grassland, the field vole is undoubtedly aptly named. However, its alternative name of short-tailed vole is also appropriate because its tail rarely reaches 30 per cent of the length of the head and body. The field vole's scientific name, *Microtus agrestis*, is fitting, too. It means 'small-eared [creature] of the fields', and this species has ears that are so short they barely emerge above the fur of the head.

The field vole has distinctive teeth, which have evolved to tackle grass. All voles have teeth with a zigzag pattern on their surfaces, but in the field vole this is more pronounced. It creates a lot of very sharp edges on the animals' teeth that help to shred grass – a much tougher food than the herbage consumed by bank voles.

The weasel

Sniffing the air to detect the scent of its prey, the weasel hunts by day and by night all year round. Such a small animal must eat every few hours to keep up its energy.

Britain's smallest carnivore, the weasel has a slender, sinuous body and is rarely more than 23cm (9in) long from nose to tail. Females often weigh as little as 50g (1½oz), and even large males weigh less than 200g (7oz). Their small size means that it is not easy to mistake weasels for other carnivores. They are also distinguished by a coat that is chestnut or russet on the upperside, and by their bright, glittering black eyes. Weasels have short legs and usually keep close to the ground,

staying under cover to avoid potential predators. They adopt a more conspicuous, bounding gait when running from one foraging patch to another. Alert and active, they spend much of their time searching for food. Although they catch most of their prey on the ground, they are also expert climbers and swimmers.

The weasel's closest relative in the mustelid family is the stoat. Although it is a small predator, the stoat is two to three times the size of the weasel.

It is also distinguished from the weasel by its much longer tail, which is usually 9–10cm (3½– 4in) long with a bristling black tip. There is a sharper, more regular line between the brown fur of most stoats' upperparts and the white fur of their underparts than in the weasel.

Although they are closely related, stoats often steal food from weasels and may even kill them. Despite their aggressive reputation, weasels are often preyed on by other, larger carnivores. Foxes, cats and owls, as

▶ *The diminutive weasel often seeks the cover of tall grass. A hunter itself, it is also the target of larger mammals, such as foxes, as well as birds of prey.*

Small weasels

Only the common weasel lives in Britain. A rarer, much smaller weasel, known as a 'mouse hunter' or 'cane', was once thought to be a separate species but, in fact, is just a small common weasel. The least weasel, found in North America, is the world's smallest carnivore.

In Britain the smaller individuals are usually females, which can be less than half the size of males. Females are rarely seen, not just because of their size but because they tend to stay in a limited area. Males have larger territories and wander more freely. Smaller weasels seen in winter may well be late-born young that have not yet fully grown.

well as stoats, all prey on weasels. It is therefore not just hunting for their own food that keeps weasels active. They must be alert constantly to ensure that they evade predators.

EFFECTIVE HUNTERS

In competing for food, weasels have an advantage over larger carnivores. In the course of millions of years, they have evolved a physique that allows them to occupy a unique niche in the food chain. A wiry, serpentine body allows them to pursue small prey into burrows or holes. Thanks to their narrow heads, weasels can squeeze into the smallest of nooks and crannies, and follow rodents down their tunnels. Once they have cornered their prey, they kill it with a fatal bite from their powerful jaws and needle-sharp teeth. Weasels have tiny, but lethal canine teeth, which they use to dislocate the bones in a mouse's or a vole's neck so that death is instantaneous.

MOUSE CATCHERS

In parts of Egypt, weasels live almost entirely in the company of humans. As efficient killers of mice and other rodents, they are regarded there more affectionately than in Britain. Before the domestication of cats, weasels were valued as rodent controllers in ancient Greece and Rome, too.

Since then, weasels have been transported around the world by humans, not always with the anticipated results. During the 1880s, for example, weasels and stoats were introduced to New Zealand in an attempt to control rabbits. The plan was a disaster as the newly rehomed predators ignored the rabbits and preyed instead on birds, including the flightless kiwis and kakapos.

MAKING TRACKS

Although weasels are rarely seen, except for the briefest instant, they are probably Britain's most numerous wild carnivore. Although absent from

Wary exit

After a hunting expedition, the weasel leaves a hole cautiously in case it attracts the attention of a predator. It is alert for larger predatory mammals or birds of prey that attack from above.

Ireland and most offshore islands, including the Isle of Man and the Channel Islands, weasels survive in all sorts of places around Britain. Preferring to be wherever their prey is plentiful, they inhabit grassland, farmland, woodland, sand dunes, marshes and moors. Occasionally, weasels may even move into urban areas if an abundant supply of rodents lives there, too. They are least likely to live in dense woodland, with little ground cover, or at higher altitudes where food is scarce.

Field signs of these tiny animals are particularly hard to find. Their tracks have a distinctive five-toed outline, but are barely 1cm (½in) in diameter and are only rarely seen in snow or mud.

However, weasel droppings – known as scats – are deposited in conspicuous places, such as on rocks and logs. They are 3–6cm (1¼–2½in) long, very thin and twisted with fur and feather remains mixed in. Scats are an important means of social communication between weasels, but they are so small that they often go unnoticed by humans.

BREEDING CAPACITY

Before the breeding season starts each year, there are probably around 450,000 weasels in Britain. Unlike most other predators, weasels are fast breeders and their numbers can increase rapidly over the year if there is enough food available. They can breed in the same year they are born, females becoming sexually mature at three to four months of age. When food is plentiful, they can have two litters a year. A single female produces an average of four to six young, called kits, per litter. If these all breed successfully in the same year, the local weasel population can increase more than 30-fold by the end of the season. For a carnivore, this is an unusually high reproductive rate.

Varied prey

Weasels are specialist rodent predators but they will also eat rabbits, especially the young ones that are plentiful in spring when mice and voles are scarce. They only occasionally eat rats and squirrels, and even fewer shrews. This is probably because shrews have an unpleasant taste.

Weasels are also accomplished raiders of nestboxes, and they particularly target those inhabited by blue tits and great tits. Their slender bodies allow weasels to squeeze into a nestbox opening of only 3cm (1¼in) across. They are most likely to climb to forage for food when rodents are scarce, or when the nesting birds are particularly numerous. Individuals are able to memorise the layout of their territories and soon learn the position of all the nestboxes in a wood.

The small rodents that live in fields and hedges offer weasels the rich supply of food they need if their numbers are to grow. Britain's weasels eat well over 200 million field voles every year, and field voles account for one third of their diet. As weasels consume such vast numbers of rodents, they are a

◄ *On average, weasels are 18–21cm (7–8¼in) long. The weasel is often seen 'periscoping' – standing on its hind legs to obtain a better view of its surroundings.*

potentially useful means by which humans might control certain rodent pests.

FRENETIC LIFESTYLE

Despite their hunting prowess, weasels are the first predators to suffer should food be in short supply. Due to their extremely small size, their energy reserves – which take the form of tiny pockets of fat along the spine and under the skin – are limited. Weasels do not slow down their lifestyle to conserve energy,

even in the harshest winter. Their heart rate is about 450 beats a minute and their metabolism is incredibly rapid. Food passes through the gut in just three hours, so weasels must eat regularly throughout the day and night just to stay alive. In total, they need to consume about a third of their own weight every day, typically 25g (1oz) for an average female or smaller male. If weasels go without food for more than a few hours, they may starve.

Myth and folklore

Possibly because they are rarely seen, a great deal of folklore surrounds weasels. In parts of western England, they were once associated with tales about fairies. It was believed that hares were hunted at night by packs of little fairy hounds called 'dandy dogs'. One interpretation of this folklore was that the dandy dogs were, in fact, weasels that had ganged together at night to pursue their larger prey. The idea of gangs of weasels is perpetuated in *The Wind in the Willows*, but weasels actually congregate only in a family group.

Tame weasels were frequently kept in the house to keep it free from rats and mice. One medieval writer suggested sprinkling weasel hair over cheese to protect it from rodents. Another recommended spreading the ashes of an incinerated weasel over gardens to scare away mice and voles.

Most bizarre of all, ancient bestiaries, encyclopedias of animals written by medieval monks, discussed whether weasels conceived through their ears and gave birth through their mouths or vice versa. These early naturalists also thought that weasels had healing

powers so that, if their young were killed, parents could bring their offspring back to life miraculously.

In Ireland, where there are no weasels, the stoat is always known colloquially as a 'weasel'. The absence of true weasels is a mystery. It is possible that weasels arrived in Britain after Ireland had already split away from the mainland. However, some biologists think that the Irish weasel population may have depended upon cold-adapted lemmings for food and, when these became extinct and were not replaced by voles, the weasels simply died out.

◀ *A few hours of activity are interspersed with a rest before the weasel is once more out and about looking for more prey. As the weasel – particularly the male – roams over a large area in search of food, it uses several dens within its territory.*

weasel numbers may plummet, with only a few individuals surviving. After conditions improve, weasels are adept at moving back into areas in which they had previously been extinct, and flourishing once more.

RISK OF PARASITES

Weasels are not only in danger from predators and starvation. Although diseases seem rare, they are susceptible to a range of parasites. Fleas and ticks are often picked up when the weasels make themselves at home in the nests of their prey. The most damaging infections are caused by a nematode (roundworm) known as *Skrjabingylus*. This destructive parasite moves from one host to another throughout its lifecycle.

Weasels must also maintain energy supplies to breed. Although males take no part in rearing their young, they patrol large territories and defend their rights to the potential mates that live there. For females, there are the combined demands of pregnancy, producing milk and keeping the kits warm, as well as feeding themselves. If vole numbers are low, many females will fail to breed as a result.

This means that weasel populations are highly volatile. In some years there can be a glut of food and the population expands rapidly. Then the next year, perhaps after a particularly cold winter,

Testing the air

Active at night as well as in daylight, the weasel discovers the whereabouts of its prey largely through smell. To pick up the scent of a potential meal it needs to raise itself above any ground vegetation. The weasel also listens carefully for the faintest sounds.

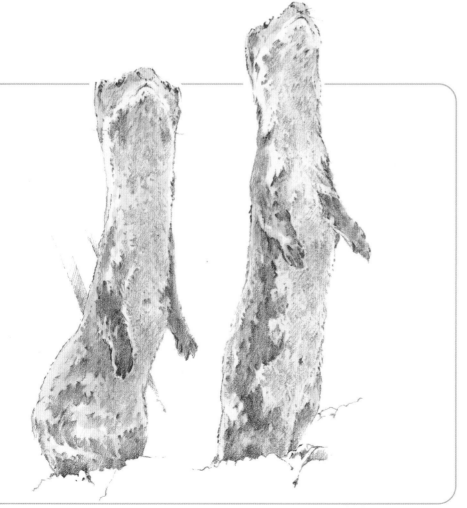

▲ *Voles and mice can form as much as 80 per cent of the weasel's diet in some places and seasons. The weasel catches a small rodent by ambushing and leaping on it, or pursuing it into its hole.*

The worms generally begin life in a mollusc host, such as a snail or slug, then move into a mouse or shrew before being eaten by a weasel. The worm larvae migrate through the weasel's body until they reach the brain. There they grow into reddish worms, up to 1cm (½in) long, which wriggle inside the weasel's skull. The worms erode the bones gradually and must cause the weasel great pain, perhaps even killing it. Between 70 and 100 per cent of weasels in some areas are infected with this parasite, which may be a major cause of death in weasel populations. Weasels are generally very short-lived for carnivores, averaging eight to nine months.

BAD REPUTATION

In Britain, weasels have long been maligned. Commonly used terms, such as 'weasel words', spread the belief that weasels are sly and devious. 'Weaselling out of things' is synonymous with double-dealing and 'weaselly' is taken to mean treacherous. In reality, the weasel is a fast, miniature hunter – sleek, curious and bold beyond its size. The result of millions of years of evolution, it is perfectly adapted to a particularly challenging role – that of nature's expert mouse catcher.

Weasels have no legal protection in Britain. Traditionally, gamekeepers have set traps for weasels and other predators that prey on game chicks. However, weasels probably kill very few of these chicks, and trapping has no long-term effect because the animals are so resilient.

The common shrew

Long, delicate whiskers and a keen sense of smell help the common shrew to find its way around its territory. Shrill squeaks may be heard when one of these tiny mammals inadvertently strays into another's domain.

Even though it is one of Britain's most abundant mammals, the common shrew is rarely seen because it spends most of its time underground. It forages for insects and earthworms in the soil or leaf litter, scurrying along tiny tunnels and runways that it digs for itself or that have been made by other small mammals.

The common shrew's most readily identifiable feature is its long and pointed snout. This seems to be in constant motion, seeking out the scent of potential prey under stones and in between leaves and grasses. Shrews have small ears and poor eyesight and in the dark depths of their tunnels they rely heavily on their sense of smell.

IDENTIFYING SHREWS

While it is easy to recognise a shrew, it is harder to decide which of the three British mainland species it is – water, pygmy or common. Water shrews can be identified by the colour of their fur, which is black above and silvery white below. Separating pygmy shrews from common shrews is more difficult, although the pygmy shrew is smaller. In pygmy shrews, the tail is at least three-quarters as long as the head and body, while the tails of common shrews are always less than half the

length of the head and body. In all shrews the sexes look similar, especially the juveniles, and a magnifying glass is necessary to tell males from females.

POWERFUL SCENT

The bodies of common shrews are often found lying on footpaths, displaying no obvious cause of death. This has been interpreted as 'dying of shock' and the shrew has a reputation for being highly strung and sensitive. It is a widespread belief that a thunderstorm will cause them

to die of fright. In fact, shrews are robust creatures and certainly no more likely to die of fright than any other creature, including humans. The reason so many are found in this way is that predators find shrews' powerful scent glands distasteful. A fox, for example, may successfully pursue and catch a shrew, but will then discard it because it tastes so unpleasant. Likewise, a cat may also catch and kill a shrew but will rarely eat it.

Shrews' scent glands are oval-shaped structures, positioned on

▶ *A shrew sniffs the air for prey, but in doing so risks some danger to itself. Shrews rarely come out into the open because they are easily snatched by predatory birds, especially owls.*

◄ *An earthworm is a favourite item in the common shrew's diet. It may struggle to eat a large worm such as this, but will not resist the challenge because the prize is enough food to last for several hours.*

their flanks, about midway between the fore and hind limbs. The glands produce a greasy, sweaty substance, which the shrew smears on to any twigs or stones it brushes against. The substance gives the animals a distinctive odour, even to a human's relatively poorly developed sense of smell. The unpleasant scent is usually enough to put off predators such as weasels and stoats, as well as foxes and many other carnivores, but birds of prey generally have a bad sense of smell and are not deterred. Shrews often form up to a third or more of the prey (by numbers) eaten by barn owls, for example.

FEROCIOUS FIGHTERS

Shrews are solitary animals and very belligerent towards each other. Indeed, a common sign of the presence of shrews is their loud and piercing squeaks when they meet each other in the undergrowth and engage in noisy confrontations.

Often the two opponents will rear up on their hind legs and scratch at each other, squeaking violently all the time, while baring their red-tipped teeth. Sometimes they grapple, rolling over and over together. When one shrew runs away, the other may pursue it, aiming bites at the retreating shrew's rump and tail. Such open aggression stems

from the fact that shrews are not sociable creatures. Each one has its own home territory and keeps itself to itself.

An individual shrew's territory comprises around 500 square metres (5400 square feet), perhaps a little less in winter, which it fiercely defends against other shrews. It will remain on its own patch throughout its short life. The marks left on stones, twigs and burrows by its strong scent glands probably serve as warning signs to keep intruders away.

In spring, though, usually in March, the shrew relaxes its territorial instincts a little so that breeding can take place. Male shrews venture into the territories of nearby females, while females become more tolerant of visitors but only for a short time. There is no real courtship and mating is not a prolonged affair. The male and female shrew separate immediately after copulating and probably never meet again. The female will aggressively rebuff any more males that approach her until she is ready to mate again.

To get a better grip during mating, the male often grasps the female by the scruff of the neck with his teeth. This sometimes damages her hair follicles so that although new fur grows, the replacement hairs lack any colour and are a distinguishing pure white. The tuft of white hair, or the scars, that many adult females display on the back of the neck are evidence of previous matings.

Fast food

The shrew lives at a hectic pace, burning a huge amount of energy, which it replenishes by eating plenty of worms and insects. It takes only short periods of rest because if a mere three hours should pass between meals, it would die of starvation.

▲ *The common shrew spends much of its time underground searching for food. It rarely has far to look as the soil teems with worms, woodlice, beetles and a host of other tiny creatures that make up this animal's diet. The shrew locates its prey by scent.*

Fighting off outsiders

Shrews share runways in the undergrowth with voles and other rodents. However, a chance encounter with another shrew from outside their own family quickly turns into a fierce battle.

▶ *Juvenile shrews have a short summer coat which becomes paler on the belly. There is less of a sharp demarcation line between the fur of the upper and lower body than in adults.*

CARAVAN OF SHREWS

Female common shrews can give birth to as many as 10 young, but litters of six or seven are more common. The babies are born pink, blind and without fur, but even at this stage they have a distinctively long snout. At 16 days old their eyes open, and at three weeks they are beginning to feed themselves. At this time, the young may leave the nest in a 'caravan'. The mother leads her family, each youngster hanging on by its teeth to the rump of the one in front. In another week, the young leave for good.

Only about a quarter of young shrews survive to breed. Most die when very young. Despite this, in the summer 50 or more common shrews may inhabit a hectare (2½ acres) of woodland or thick grassland. Later in the year, however, the death of the adult generation, coupled with high juvenile mortality, reduces numbers by more than half.

In one summer, a female may have up to four litters, although one or two is more usual. By the end of the season, about September, the females are exhausted and most die soon

afterwards. Shortly after this, most males reach the end of their natural lifespan and they, too, die. Only a tiny percentage of animals live to be one year old and none exceeds 23 months in the wild. The species survives over winter thanks to the juveniles born the previous summer.

CHANGING FUR PATTERNS

When they become independent, juvenile shrews are a pale brown all over. Come the autumn, they begin to moult their summer coat of short hairs, which is replaced by a new longer and darker coat of sleek fur for the winter. By November, the animal is dark chocolate-brown, almost black, with a distinct contrast between the paler fur of the belly and darker back. In the spring, this fur is shed and replaced by a shorter

summer coat, which is also dark in colour. The tail hairs are not moulted and regrown, so the tail gets steadily more hairless as the animal gets older and hairs are worn off it. This helps to distinguish adults from juveniles, which have a comparatively hairy tail like that of the pygmy shrew.

Another puzzling development occurs in the autumn. Instead of fattening up for the winter as most mammals do, shrews shrink by a quarter. Even their skull and bones get smaller, then regain full size the following year. Exactly how they manage this feat is uncertain and its biological significance is obscure. However, the weight loss obviously does them no harm, since enough shrews always manage to survive to repopulate the countryside in the spring.

CHAPTER 2 • WOODLAND AND COPPICE

The badger

Superbly adapted to their underground lifestyle, these instantly recognisable animals were once in sharp decline. Now that they are fully protected by the law, their numbers are increasing every year.

Until a few decades ago, little was known about the habits of badgers – although large and distinctive, they were considered reclusive creatures of the night, unlikely to be encountered up close. But badgers had good reason to be shy of human contact. In addition to generations of persecution by game-keepers, their setts, as their burrow systems are called, were regularly disrupted by badger baiters seeking to pit fierce dogs against them – an illegal activity then, as now.

Fortunately, things are very different today. The badger has a large number of ardent supporters, with numerous badger groups around the country working to monitor their local populations and

► *Viewed head-on, the badger's facial pattern is unmistakable. The eyes are relatively small and so are the white-tipped ears. Long whiskers protrude from either side of the mouth and nose.*

Curious stripes

The badger is grizzled grey on its back, with a black underside and legs. The face is white with a broad black stripe up each side over the eye – but why? Badgers are not only nocturnal but also subterranean, so what purpose can a striped face serve? Why are they not black, or grey, all over?

One suggestion is that these markings actually make the animal harder to see in the dappled shadows caused by moonlight filtering through the trees.

Another, less plausible suggestion is that the striped face may be easier to see underground, allowing badgers to recognise each other. The problem with this idea is that total darkness reigns underground at night and nothing can be seen at all. Moreover, badgers are known to recognise other individuals by scent, not by sight.

It has also been suggested that the black and white stripes serve as a warning, but to whom? Badgers do not have any significant natural predators. Few other animals would attempt to tackle such a large creature, especially one armed with such long claws and powerful jaws. No one seems to know.

observe them in their natural environment. Much of this change came about through the books of the late Dr Ernest Neal. An English schoolmaster and naturalist, Dr Neal described how anyone could enjoy the thrill of watching badgers in the wild, with no special equipment beyond a torch and perhaps some insect repellent. Thanks to his work, and more enlightened attitudes to wildlife in general, badgers now have legal protection, which also extends to their setts. This is one reason why badger numbers have steadily increased and continue to do so.

In some areas, there may be up to 10 badgers per square kilometre (26 per square mile) and more in

parts of south-west England. The reason for such success is not certain, but moist climate and plentiful pastureland, and therefore earthworms – part of their staple diet – may be important factors. Badgers are quite rare in upland areas, where the soil is often waterlogged or rocky below the surface. They are also relatively scarce in East Anglia – perhaps not fully recovered from the persecution they once suffered there.

EARTH MOVERS

With their powerful limbs and big claws, badgers are great diggers, and they excavate extensive burrows in soft, sandy soils. The sett may comprise hundreds of metres (yards)

These badgers are grooming each other, a behaviour that serves not only to strengthen the bond between them, but also to spread scent from one to the other, thereby ensuring that members of a social group can all recognise each other by smell.

A badger's front feet are powerful digging implements that can rapidly move large quantities of earth. The claws cannot be retracted and they make dangerous weapons with which the animal can defend itself if necessary.

of tunnels, dug out by successive generations of badgers.

Each paw is armed with long curved claws on all five toes, and the bones of the shoulder and forelimbs are modified to make best use of the powerful arm muscles, providing leverage for shifting stones and earth. Digging is done with the broad forepaws – loose earth is scooped backwards under the belly, and kicked away with the smaller hind feet.

The badger's fur is coarse and wiry with widely spaced hairs. Each hair is about 5–7cm (2–3in) long, white tipped and rather crinkly. Hairs caught on barbed-wire fences as the badger squeezes beneath are easy to identify.

Cosy bedding

It is cool underground and possibly damp as well, so in order to make the sett more comfortable badgers bring in large amounts of bedding in the form of dry grass, bracken or other suitable dry vegetation. They rake up the grass using their front paws, tuck a bundle between their forearms and chin and shuffle backwards to the sett, dragging it underground. The untidy trail left by this activity is a clue to the location of a badger sett.

Badgers are scrupulously clean animals and always leave the sett to use a special toilet area outside, rather than fouling their nests. Nevertheless, the bedding gets soggy after a few months and badgers usually clean it out at the end of winter, leaving a large heap outside the sett.

A powerful bite

Badgers have a basically carnivorous dentition, but the molar teeth are broad and knobbly for grinding up tough nuts and gritty worms. The jaws have such a strong hinge that they cannot be detached, even in a clean skull, that is one from which all hair and flesh have been removed – no other British mammal has such firmly attached jaws. The skull has a high crest along its ridge to provide increased area for the attachment of enlarged jaw muscles. All this enables the badger to deliver the most powerful bite of any British mammal, said to be strong enough to leave dents in a metal spade.

Unlike the majority of mammals, badgers lack dense, fine underfur. A coarse coat is better suited to life underground – it protects the skin from damage, but does not become clogged with soil and mud and is easily cleaned with some vigorous scratching. When badgers venture above ground each evening, they spend a lot of time grooming the soil out of their coats.

The wiry fur does not provide much insulation, but the large amount of fat accumulated beneath the skin does the same job and helps to keep them warm. This fat is also useful as a food reserve. Badgers were once thought to hibernate through winter food shortages, but it is now known that they are not true hibernators. However, they do remain inactive underground during long periods of inclement weather, relying on their fat reserves to tide them over until conditions improve.

◄ *Scraping tree trunks or stumps helps to clean the badger's long claws. It may also be a form of territorial marking, leaving scent, as well as scratches, on the wood as a message to other badgers.*

▶ *It is not unknown for badgers to drink in hot weather, although their food normally contains enough moisture. Look for their distinctive footprints in the mud near water, particularly ditches where crossing points have been identified.*

A visit to a sett after a snowfall will usually show footprints in the snow, confirming that the badgers are still awake. This is the ideal time to note a curiosity in their tracks – because the hind feet are smaller than the front feet, footprints from a single animal can often look like two animals of different sizes walking in single file.

NOCTURNAL ACTIVITY

Badgers emerge from the sett each evening at dusk, about the time the last birds stop singing, and after grooming, they set off to feed, usually alone. They rely mainly on smell to find their way about and locate good feeding places – badgers' eyesight is fairly poor and cubs are especially short-sighted. Usually, they trot or amble around with a rolling gait, slowing to sniff around carefully in promising areas for food. If alarmed, badgers can show a surprising burst of speed, sprinting off at up to 30 kilometres per hour (18mph) over short distances. They can also climb, using their claws and powerful forelimbs to grip rough stonework or the bark of logs. Sloping trees are often explored and badger hairs may be found more than three metres (10ft) above the ground.

▶ *Badgers sometimes feed as a group when a concentration of tasty food is found outside the sett. This may include peanuts or raisins, scattered there by hopeful badger watchers.*

FEEDING HABITS

Badgers belong to the same family as weasels and stoats, the Mustelidae, which also includes otters, mink and polecats. These are all predatory animals and, like their relatives, badgers eat small mammals and frogs, and will relish a nest full of baby rabbits or birds' eggs. They will kill and eat hedgehogs too – their long claws and strong forelimbs enable them to prise open even a tightly rolled hedgehog, an impossible task for most other predators. Hedgehogs are rarely found in large populations when many badgers are present and, in some areas, badgers can be a significant threat to the continued survival of the local hedgehog population.

The badger does, however, have a wide-ranging diet and also eats a lot of smaller creatures. For instance, badgers will eagerly dig out wasp nests or nests of solitary bees to feast on their larvae and any stores of honey that might be present, their long coarse fur protecting them from retaliatory stings. Invertebrates such as earthworms and beetles are nutritious, yet do not require much effort to catch.

Earthworms in particular play an important part in the badger's diet, although their contribution varies from place to place. The availability of worms may be one of the factors that limits badger numbers in certain parts of the country, and may also affect population density and social group structure. In dry weather, worms stay deep and inactive in the soil, so long periods of drought can cause serious problems for badgers, especially cubs – many will die in a long, hot summer. It is likely that Britain's warm, wet summers, especially in the south-west, have helped badgers reach their present high numbers, but a few long dry summers could still result in a significant population crash.

VARIED DIET

Although carnivorous, badgers will supplement their diet with vegetable matter, including bluebell bulbs, wild

Badgers and TB

The rise in badger numbers has unfortunately brought them into conflict with farmers, who accuse them of infecting cattle with bovine tuberculosis. The badger is legally protected, but some farmers want the authority to control them by culling, and this has generated a simmering controversy to rival the debate over foxhunting.

Badgers can certainly contract bovine tuberculosis (TB) in laboratory experiments and in the wild – the first badger TB victim was discovered in 1971. Farmers claim that they spread the disease among cattle by physical contact and in urine on pastures. They say there is a link between the badger population boom of the past few decades and the rise in TB in their herds. However, conservationists argue that these claims ignore everything that is known about badger habits – they usually steer well clear of larger animals – and point out that the rise in TB also coincided with increasing industrialisation of farming. They say that TB outbreaks in previously clean herds are far more likely to originate from new cattle shipped in over long distances than from distinctly stay-at-home badgers.

Successive governments have conducted studies into the problem, but with badger population and distribution still little understood, they have had difficulty coming up with any definite conclusions.

arum corms and, in rural areas, even garden bulbs in the spring. Fruits, such as blackberries and bilberries in upland areas and fallen apples in orchards and gardens, are a favourite in the autumn. Beech mast (the fruit of beech trees) and acorns are also relished.

Their plant-eating habits can lead badgers into raiding cereal crops, where they not only consume the grain, but also roll in the ripening corn, making it difficult to harvest properly. They are particularly fond of maize and the increasing prevalence of this crop in modern farming is another probable factor in the badger's rising numbers.

RAISING YOUNG

Badgers do not normally breed until they are at least two years old, although earlier breeding is not unknown. They mate during spring, but the development of the embryos is delayed for many weeks before normal pregnancy starts. The cubs – up to five – may be born any time from January to April but mostly they arrive in February, which ensures that when they leave the sett eight weeks later, food is plentiful.

At first, the cubs have pink skin covered with a thin layer of silky white fur, and the facial stripes are barely visible. The milk teeth do

not appear for a month or so, and the cubs spend their first eight weeks underground, slowly growing into miniature versions of their parents.

When the nights at last start to get warmer, the young make their first appearance above ground. They still depend on their mother for milk at this stage and are not weaned until about 12 weeks old. If food is scarce, they can take milk for much longer, and may not be fully weaned for four to six months. However, normally they grow quickly, especially if there are plenty of worms available, and can weigh as much as 10kg (22lb) by the end of their first year. Young badgers have little to fear from predators –

▲ *Cubs spend several weeks underground before they first emerge in spring Their characteristic short, blunt muzzles elongate with age until, at about eight months old, their faces resemble those of their parents.*

dogs may kill a few, foxes may occasionally snatch a very young unprotected cub and adult badgers have been known to kill them occasionally. Nevertheless, about 50 per cent of cubs do not survive to one year old.

Annual road deaths may be as high as 10,000, and inexperienced cubs are particularly at risk of being run over, as are young badgers in areas of high population density, as they roam in search of new feeding places.

Youthful high spirits

Play among young badger cubs probably helps to cement the bonds within the social group. This becomes important as they grow older, when they will spread out to forage alone each night before returning to the sett.

The roe deer

The shy roe deer prefers to graze near woodland thickets, but sometimes ventures out into the open to feed under cover of darkness. It is easiest to spot in summer when its coat turns bright russet brown.

While red deer and fallow deer may be readily seen in deer parks, roe deer are not normally kept in captivity. They are less placid in temperament than other deer and are most likely to be seen alone, or in a family group of a female, called a doe, with one or two young, or kids.

COAT COLOURS

The roe deer is smaller than the red or fallow deer, and in summer can be easily recognised by its bright reddish brown coat, which moults to a darker greyish brown in winter. No other British deer displays such a contrast between its summer and winter coats.

The coat hairs, which are stiff and bristly, grow up to 50 per cent longer in winter, and this somewhat shaggier coat makes the roe deer look stockier and shorter-legged than in summer. They look even scruffier when they moult from around Easter onwards,

but by June they have grown their rufous summer coat. The roe deer's fairly short face gives it an alert appearance, and it has a distinctive black, pointed muzzle with a contrasting bright white chin.

Another identifying characteristic is its rump, which the deer displays when it takes fright and runs for cover. The roe deer is easily alarmed. Unlike fallow deer, there is no black on the roe deer's tail. In fact, it is quite difficult to perceive any tail at all as it is very short – only about 5cm (2in) in length – and white so that it blends in with the patch of pale fur that surrounds it. In addition to this, the female has a tuft of long pale fur hanging from the rump.

CROWN OF SPIKES

The male roe deer – called a 'buck', not a stag – carries short, spiky antlers, which do not grow beyond about 25cm (10in) at most. In common with most deer, the female

has no antlers. Unlike other deer, the buck's antlers have a rough, knobbly surface to their main stem, which looks as if it is thickly encrusted with brown cement. The prongs, or tines, that branch off from this are smooth and there are normally only two or three on each antler.

Bucks have a well-developed coronet, which is a thickened ring where the antler rises from a bony stalk on the skull. This stalk, called a pedicle, may be visible when the kid is just four months old.

Antlers are shed and regrown during the winter. The new antlers form inside a protective covering of woolly skin, referred to as velvet, that is shed around April time. Bucks often thrash their heads against trees

▼ *Roe deer can run at impressive speed, reaching about 32km/h (20mph) at full gallop, their bodies outstretched. When threatened, a buck's flight reaction is instant.*

◀ *At about two years old, a buck claims a territory that it will occupy until ousted by a younger male. In late May, when the antlers are hard and fully grown, the buck rubs the glands on its head against trees and shrubs to leave scent to warn off rivals.*

or shrubs to assist in freeing the antlers from their furry sheaths, and in doing so, spread scent from their facial glands. This sends a territorial signal to other deer in the area.

Curiously, some bucks fail to rid themselves of the velvet, or to cast their antlers, and the coverings remain, thickening with each passing year. This may be due to low levels of the male hormone testosterone in the blood. Bucks that keep their velvet are referred to as having a 'perruque' head. ('Perruque' is French for 'wig'.)

The male grows a first set of antlers, which form a single short spike, at about nine months old. Each new set is larger than the previous one until the antlers reach their maximum size. The size of the antlers, and their number of points, is not a reliable guide to the age of roe deer because their antlers are never very large, tending to become thick rather than long. However, the thickest antlers are likely to belong to deer more than three years old.

FOREST COVER

Roe deer normally live in woodland, but they sometimes wander on to open moors, even those high in the mountains of Scotland. They will live on farmland and raid crops, but usually only where there are nearby forests and thickets to which they can run for cover. Roe deer thrive in young forestry plantations at the stage just before the trees form a dense thicket and are thinned out. Here the deer population may increase so that there are more than 20 per square kilometre (52 per square mile).

As the trees grow they cast an increasingly dense shadow, throwing the shrubs and grasses on which the deer feed into deep shade where they cannot flourish. As a result, older forests do not provide enough food for the high numbers of deer that a young plantation can support. This is especially true of conifer plantations where, as the trees get taller, the lower branches die back, so that the nourishing parts grow out of reach of deer. The number of deer living in such plantations may halve by the time the trees are about 20 years old.

FEEDING HABITS

Roe deer generally feed about nine times in the course of 24 hours. They are ruminants and so, after eating, they rest and regurgitate their food, chewing it thoroughly again. After that, the food passes through several stomach chambers to the gut. Roe

Fleeing fast

A roe deer may be tempted into the open in daylight by its favourite food – brambles, for instance, growing in a woodland clearing. If disturbed when browsing, though, the deer will immediately take flight.

deer often feed in the half light of dawn and dusk, but their behaviour is influenced by disturbance. Where there is a lot of human activity, the deer are likely to be largely nocturnal, and spend the day hidden in dense cover.

DEFENDING TERRITORY

In summer, bucks mostly live alone, fending off intruders. The does may stay in a small family group with their young from the previous year. In general, bucks are territorial from about Easter until late summer, but not all the males hold territories. Those that do not probably do not breed either. Bucks with territories bark aggressively and chase other deer away. They also mark trees and shrubs with scent to warn off trespassing rivals. It is rare for fights to occur, however.

During the winter, roe deer may live together in small groups, but they never form large herds. Bucks roam much more widely than in summer, while does tend to stay on familiar home ground. When a doe dies, its area is taken over by a younger female, usually a daughter. The home ranges of does often overlap with each other and with the larger territories of one or more bucks.

▼ *In summer, the male is in peak condition, ready for mating, coat sleek and short-pronged antlers hardened. The antlers are roughened near the base and may be bloodstained where they have been rubbed against trees and shrubs.*

On the alert

Without the security provided by the many ears, eyes and noses of a herd, roe deer are always wary. They have acute senses of smell and hearing. This doe constantly swivels her large, sensitive ears in order to detect anything remotely unusual.

UNUSUAL PREGNANCY

Roe deer mate in high summer but, uniquely among deer, the fertilised egg lies inside the female in a state of suspended development. Pregnancy does not begin until about December so that the young are not born in late winter when bad weather and little food would reduce the chance of survival. Instead, they are born from mid-May into early June when conditions are more favourable. Does often return to the same place each year to have their young. When it is time to give birth, they become solitary and aggressive towards other deer.

RAISING KIDS

Newborn kids are covered with dark brown fur and dappled with white spots. Their eyes are open and, within hours of birth, they can follow their mother as she moves about to feed. She provides them with milk for six to eight weeks while they learn to feed themselves. They may take vegetation into their mouths when they are as young as four days old, soon discarding it again. They start to eat solid food after a week. The white spots on the kids' coats fade after about six

▶ *Although roe deer often give birth to a single kid, twins are more common. Does even produce triplets occasionally, especially where food is plentiful.*

weeks, and disappear at the first moult in the autumn. Growing steadily, the young cut their permanent teeth the following year.

They now look like adults and, continuing to mature, breed for the first time at about 14 months. Young does may be allowed to remain on the edge of their mothers' home ranges but when young bucks are a year or two old, they are usually driven away by adults of both sexes, unless a buck inherits its father's territory. This is often the case as bucks rarely hold a territory for more than about three years before being succeeded by younger males.

HAZARDS OF LIFE

Many dangers threaten roe deer, even though their main natural predator – the wolf – is now extinct in Britain. Golden eagles and wildcats are also no longer a danger to kids except in some parts of Scotland. However, dogs, foxes and cars take their toll, as do parasites and disease. Kids are particularly vulnerable. More than half do not survive their first year, and nearly three-quarters die before they are old enough to breed. The average life span of roe deer is about two to three years, although some can live for 10 years or more – in rare cases up to 16 years.

The grey squirrel

In the hundred years or so since its arrival in Britain, the grey squirrel has become a common sight in woodlands and parks, sitting on tree stumps and branches to feed or running up and down tree trunks with ease.

A native of the hardwood forests of the eastern United States, the grey squirrel was deliberately introduced to Britain during the 19th and early 20th centuries. These days the introduction of foreign species is carefully controlled, but a century or so ago interest focused on adding more species to the resident fauna. Being less specialised in diet and habitat than the native red squirrel, the grey squirrel was able to thrive, displacing its once widespread smaller cousin.

Between 1930 and 1945, grey squirrels spread like wildfire across the Midlands and over most of southern England, despite efforts to control them. For a while there was

▶ *On the ground there is a wider variety of food than in the tree-tops. Ground feeding is mainly done in dry weather because grey squirrels dislike getting wet.*

Leaps and bounds

Although they are adapted for life in the trees, grey squirrels spend a lot of their time searching for food on the ground. When startled grey squirrels can move at great speed, heading for the nearest tree in a series of bounds.

▶ *In hot weather a grey squirrel sometimes drinks from a pond or stream. Squirrels are generally wary of water because they are not good swimmers; their tails are easily waterlogged, making swimming a struggle.*

an official government 'bounty' paid for every grey squirrel killed, but still the species prospered, living in woods, hedgerows and on farmland. Intelligent and adaptable, these squirrels invaded towns as well as countryside, delighting many visitors to parks with their acrobatic antics and bold character.

The spread of grey squirrels into Wales, Cornwall, East Anglia and other regions was slowed by wide expanses of treeless countryside – squirrels rarely stray far from trees – but they are now well established in all these areas. Populations in Scotland are increasing although greys are still less numerous there than reds. Today two-and-a-half million grey squirrels are to be found in Britain, 80 per cent of them in England.

TREE DAMAGE

Squirrels are unusual among British mammals in that they are active during daylight. Unlike other animals they sit up to feed, manipulating food in their paws. This appealing behaviour adds to their attractiveness and grey squirrels are popular animals – at least among people who are not trying to protect the red squirrel or earn a living by growing trees.

Foresters dislike squirrels because they gnaw tree bark. The gnawing often occurs in patches just above a convenient side branch where the squirrel can sit. It strips off sections of bark with its sharp teeth, eats the juicy parts underneath and drops the waste to the ground below. This sort of damage not only disfigures the tree, resulting in significant losses of some hardwoods, but may cause the tree crown to die. Removal of bark also exposes the tree to the danger of fungal infections. The work and investment of several decades can be severely affected in just a few weeks by these marauding mammals.

BORN ACROBATS

The squirrel is well adapted to life in the trees, with sharp claws on each of its toes and powerful gripping feet. It is able to hang on to tiny branches in high winds, scamper up smooth bark and defy gravity by running down a tree head-first. It can also hang head downwards by its hind toes. This is made possible by having double-jointed ankles, which allow the hind feet to be turned backwards.

A squirrel's eyes face forwards, allowing accurate judgement of distances. It can leap 6m (20ft) or more and its tail acts as a balancer, flicking from side to side to help the animal avoid falling while it finds a hold with its feet.

GREY OR RED?

In summer, the grey squirrel's coat is much thinner than it is in winter and turns orange-brown along the back, flanks, legs and head. This sometimes causes confusion with the red squirrel and people often suggest (wrongly) that perhaps the two species may interbreed to form hybrids.

▲ *Grey squirrels appear to relish the challenge of reaching food meant for birds and the rewards are rich indeed – nuts and seeds usually shelled and ready for eating.*

In fact, grey squirrels can be distinguished from reds, which are a bright chestnut colour, in a number of ways. Firstly, grey squirrels are larger and more heavily built than red squirrels. Secondly, the grey squirrel's tail has a dark core with a white fringe, while the red squirrel's tail is the same chestnut colour throughout. Yet another way to distinguish between the two species is to look at their ears – the red squirrel has long tufts of hair at the tips of its ears, while the grey squirrel does not.

HOME SWEET HOME

Squirrels build nests, called dreys, from twigs bitten off a living tree. Each twig bears some green leaves which, although they become shrivelled, remain attached to the twigs. As a result, the typical squirrel drey has a bushy assortment of leaves visible on the outside. Magpies build similar-sized nests – a little larger than a football – but use dead twigs, so their nests do not have leaves visible on the outside.

The interior of a drey is lined with soft material such as moss or finely shredded bark. The summer drey is often little more than a platform of twigs, often constructed among the thin branches at the top of a tree. In winter, with no leaves on the tree, such a position would be too exposed to the elements, so winter dreys are more robust and built closer to the tree trunk or in substantial tree forks.

Outside the breeding season, squirrels may share dreys or visit nests built and used previously by other individuals. They will also take up residence in old woodpecker holes or tree hollows, enlarging the entrance as necessary by gnawing away bark and wood.

Squirrels do not hibernate but they often remain inactive in their nests for many days if the weather is cold and wet. On sunny days they will be out seeking food, even in the snow.

FOOD GLORIOUS FOOD

In spring, the squirrels feed mainly up in the trees on the buds of developing leaves. They also scamper through the branches, sniffing at flowers to select those that are at the right stage of development, when they are highly nutritious, before biting them off to eat.

In summer, they eat increasing quantities of insects, including caterpillars, which are often abundant in the tree canopy. They will also eat birds' eggs, if they find them, but squirrels do not appear to make special efforts to seek out nests and eggs, nor is it likely that these raids have a significant effect on bird numbers.

Later in the year they eat acorns, beech mast and all sorts of seeds and fruits, as well as fungi. Squirrels are especially fond of hazelnuts and bite them off the tree branches while they are still green. However, all sorts of nuts drop to the ground when ripe and grey squirrels take advantage of this at all times of year, especially in autumn and winter, when they spend up to 75 per cent of their time feeding on the ground rather than in the trees. The squirrels scurry about, sniffing the ground to detect food or spotting a potential meal with their keen eyesight.

They will pick up nuts, swiftly discarding those that do not weigh enough – squirrels learn by experience to distinguish between worthless shells, where the nuts have been eaten from the inside by insects, and those that contain a nice solid kernel. Squirrels strip chestnuts and acorns of their outer coverings, whereas hazelnuts have to be gnawed until the squirrel can insert the tips of its incisor teeth and split the nutshell apart.

Some smaller nuts may be cracked in the squirrel's jaws. The shells are left in jagged pieces and look quite different from the nuts opened by mice and dormice, which have a neat hole in the shell where the rodents have gnawed them.

NUT LARDERS

In the autumn there is often too much to eat all at once, so squirrels store food, collecting nuts and burying them all over the place. They do not remember where they hide their larders but they do recognise the patches of ground used for this purpose. Later they return and seek out the nuts by smell and by

▶ *Grey squirrels feed heartily during summer and autumn. Their success in finding food at this time crucially affects their survival over winter and breeding success the following year.*

Tree-top skills

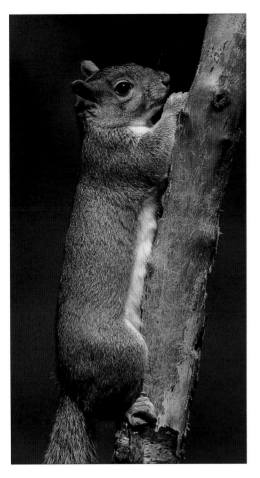

▲ *The grey squirrel uses its powerful jaws and teeth to strip off tree bark so that it can feed on the layers underneath.*

The feet of the grey squirrel are adapted both for digging and clambering in trees. The long fingers and claws are almost birdlike. The thumb of the front foot is only vestigial.

experimental digging. Of course, some nuts are never found and these are able to germinate away from the tree that produced them. So, in providing themselves with their main source of food for the winter, squirrels help to disperse tree seeds.

PINE SEED FEAST

While nuts are abundant in autumn, the seeds inside pine cones are present at all times of the year. This is another food source exploited by squirrels. They gnaw the scales off cones, eat the seeds and discard the cores, just as people throw away apple cores. These stripped cone cores, surrounded by the debris of nibbled cone scales, are a sure sign of squirrel feeding activity. Stripping a

cone takes quite some time, so the squirrels prefer to do it sitting on a prominent branch, tree stump or fencepost from where they can watch for approaching danger.

EARLY BREEDING

Food is very important in determining breeding success. In a good year, when there is plenty of autumn food, the animals start the winter in good condition and are still quite fat and well fed when the breeding season starts in January. Energetic mating chases are frequent at this time, and females will then have to invest further energy, not only in producing young, but also producing the milk to feed them. All this has to take place before much new food develops on the trees.

So, if the food supply is poor in the autumn, fewer young will be raised successfully the following spring. If the winter has been particularly harsh, the female's body will be in poor condition and many of her young will die as a result of her inability to feed them properly.

The young are born from February (or even January in the south) onwards. Up to seven babies may be produced in a single family, but three is more usual. If the mother is disturbed, she will often take her offspring to a safer place, carrying them one at a time in her mouth. The males play no part in raising the family and do not live with them.

The babies weigh 14–18g (around ½oz) at birth and are blind and helpless at this stage. They take two

▲ *Protected by a thickened coat of silvery grey, squirrels are out and about on bright days throughout the winter. They can usually find enough to eat, and can always fall back on reserves hidden away the previous autumn.*

to three weeks to grow fur and up to a month to open their eyes. A full set of teeth will have developed by around five weeks of age, but the young squirrels do not leave the nest and feed on solid food until they are around seven weeks old. They finally become independent of their mother after two-and-a-half to four months. The mother may then have a second litter, born from July onwards. All the juveniles will have left the family before the onset of winter, sometimes travelling more than 3km (2 miles).

Squirrels become mature enough to breed when they are about a year old, but many die long before this. Cats kill unwary baby squirrels, as do cars. Large numbers are run over, especially in late summer when the inexperienced juveniles are dispersing and looking for somewhere to live. Young animals facing their first winter suffer high mortality rates and more than half will die before their first birthday. Those that do survive, having learnt the dangers of predators and traffic, still have the problems of seasonal food shortages

to contend with. However, young individuals that overcome these hazards have a life expectancy of several years. The maximum lifespan in the wild is probably around ten years, although very few will reach such an age.

SQUIRREL TERRITORIES

Female grey squirrels use an area of 2–10 hectares (5–25 acres) throughout the year but males range more widely, especially in the breeding season when they are looking for mates. Population densities can sometimes be quite high, often more than two per hectare (2½ acres). This can lead to aggressive activity in the breeding season, with scent marking, growling and tail-wagging used as territorial signals to other squirrels. Violent clashes may ensue and, although fighting is unusual, this is probably the main cause of damaged ears that seem to be fairly prevalent among grey squirrels.

However, in winter, peace reigns and the animals often share nests, huddled together to keep warm. Sometimes six or more squirrels may live together in a tree hole at this time of year.

The common dormouse

As daylight fades, a dormouse curled up in its tree nest rouses itself from its slumbers. Relying on an excellent sense of smell, this agile rodent scrambles among the branches, balancing on the thinnest twigs to reach a choice morsel.

Spotting a common dormouse in the wild is never easy. Even in its active phase during the summer, the creature's nocturnal, tree-climbing habits and its general scarcity make it a rare sight indeed.

The common dormouse, which belongs to the family Gliridae, begins to come out of hibernation in April, later in the north of Britain. At first, it is awake for brief periods only but these gradually become longer until the little rodent is fully active in May, although it still sleeps during the day. It feeds on hawthorn, caterpillars and aphids, among other flowers and insects, so that it will be in peak condition for mating in late May or early June, which is late compared with other British rodents.

The young are born in July or early August when flowers and fruit are plentiful. There are normally four, but sometimes as many as seven, young in a litter. Nests have been found containing more than eight babies and this may be the result of two females sharing the workload of raising their families.

By the autumn dormice are busy fattening up for their winter hibernation. They are especially fond of hazelnuts – an alternative name for the common dormouse is hazel dormouse – as well as beech nuts and blackberries. They will also seek out yew trees to feast on their red berries.

In warm years a second brood may be born at this time, but young dormice born late in the season may not be able to find enough food to fatten up sufficiently before the first hard frosts occur. A good supply of hazelnuts and sweet chestnuts, some of the last foods to ripen in the autumn, is absolutely essential for their winter survival.

LONG SLEEP

Most dormice hibernate from October and by mid-November all will be curled up in their warm winter nests to spend the next five months or so asleep. Hibernation is a successful survival strategy. While other small mammals struggle to find food and keep warm in the cold winter climate, the dormouse sleeps through it all, living off the body fat that it has accumulated during the autumn.

The dormouse is completely inactive during hibernation, and its metabolic rate slows to almost nothing. Its body temperature drops so low that it feels cold to the touch – it is normally only a degree or two warmer than its surroundings – and its rate of respiration slows dramatically. As long as the dormouse goes into hibernation weighing at least 12–15g (about ½oz), it should have sufficient reserves to last through a long winter.

In fact, a long, cold winter provides the ideal conditions for hibernating dormice. Problems are more likely to arise if the winter is very mild. This is because the dormouse may wake up and go in search of food that is not there, wasting valuable reserves that cannot be replenished until spring. The mild winters of south-west Britain, for example, are not conducive to long periods of hibernation, which are much more likely in the drier, colder winters typical of the south-east.

◀ *Discarded hazelnut shells provide a clue to the presence of dormice. They have a unique way of opening hazelnuts, making a neat round hole with a smooth, bevelled edge to the opening. Search for them beneath the outermost branches of fruiting hazel trees and use a hand lens to check on the tooth marks. Wood mice and bank voles make toothmarks that leave a rough edge to the hole and squirrels always crack the nuts apart.*

Dormice need warm summer weather, though. If it is chilly and wet at this time of year, they tend to stay in their nests for longer, spend less time feeding and devote less time to mating and breeding. If the early summer is cool, they may even enter a state of torpor to save energy, as they do when hibernating.

LOSS OF HABITAT

About a hundred years ago, dormice were numerous all over England and Wales – hence the name 'common' dormouse. They were often found when hedges were trimmed and ditches cleaned out in winter. Children would keep them as pets. Now they are rare.

▲ *The dormouse makes the best use of whatever food is available, including berries in late summer and autumn. It has a varied diet and cannot survive on just leaves and grasses.*

There are several reasons for this but the most important is undoubtedly loss of habitat. Like many other woodland animals, they have suffered as a result of woods being cleared to make way for roads, farms and houses. Roads are a particular problem because they divide large woodlands up into smaller patches, and dormice do not like to cross roads or open spaces. They become isolated in the woods

Help dormice

Wildlife trusts manage reserves where dormice are present, and from time to time hold working parties to help regenerate derelict coppices. Volunteers are usually welcome.

Nesting boxes have proved to be very successful at helping encourage and maintain dormouse populations at known sites, so making these and donating them to reserves is of great benefit.

Searching for signs of dormice in woodlands where they are not known to occur, or where they once did occur but have not been seen recently, can help identify places that might otherwise be overlooked. Local wildlife trusts are always pleased to hear the results of such observations.

that remain and, although a copse of one hectare (2½ acres) may support up to ten adult dormice, that is too few to guarantee long-term survival.

Now naturalists and conservationists are using captive breeding programmes to re-introduce dormice to selected areas, releasing them in a controlled way to help ensure their survival.

IDEAL HOME

Dormice are well adapted for life in trees. Their long bushy tails aid balance when running along branches or when sitting on a twig. The ideal dormouse habitat

◄ *The common dormouse may spend eight hours or more in its nest every day. Spring and summer nests are made above ground in hedgerows or trees and consist mainly of shredded honeysuckle bark woven into a ball, often with an outer layer of leaves. Winter nests are normally built at ground level, often under leaf litter.*

contains a mixture of native trees and shrubs, providing a succession of fruits, seeds, nuts and berries throughout the late spring, summer and early autumn. Dense thickets of bramble and curtains of twining honeysuckle provide cover for nesting as well as additional food supplies. An interlocking growth of stems and branches enables the dormouse to clamber around in search of food without ever coming down to ground level. All it needs for nesting and survival can be found among the branches.

Curiously, pigs and dormice do not mix. Woodlands such as the New Forest that have a long tradition of 'pannage' – free-range pigs foraging among the trees in winter – now support few or none of the little mammals. The reason for the conflict is thought to be the result of the way in which pigs root around for acorns on the woodland floor. In the process they may disturb, crush or even eat hibernating dormice.

▲ *The name dormouse probably derives from the Latin 'dormire', which means to sleep – an appropriate name for a creature that spends most of its time in hibernation.*

LIFE EXPECTANCY

Owl pellets are among the best indicators of which small mammals are present in a woodland, but the remains of dormice are rarely found in them. Tawny owls do sometimes take dormice but voles and wood mice seem to be much easier prey. This may be partly because they are much more numerous. Dormice are so scarce that the chances of a predator finding them, especially when other small mammals are so abundant, are low.

Weasels sometimes take dormice, and cats occasionally catch them. However, most dormice live for two to three years – some for as long as five or more years – and die as a result of low food reserves, bad weather or disease rather than being eaten by a predator.

The fox

Adept at survival, the fox still thrives in woodlands throughout the country but has spread its territory to wherever it can find food and a safe place to raise its young.

Foxes are to be found the length and breadth of the country, from the centre of London to high up in the Cairngorms of Scotland. Successful predators and effective scavengers, they eat an extraordinarily wide range of food, including rabbits, chickens, fish, beetles, earthworms and even fruit, such as strawberries. This is one reason why, despite sustained campaigns against it, this truly remarkable animal has been able to survive and prosper in increasingly difficult circumstances.

SECRET OF SUCCESS

The real reason why the fox is able to thrive lies in its adaptability. Not being particularly specialised in its needs means that the fox is able to find food and shelter in most environments. This may be why it seems to be most abundant in places where a mixture of woods, hedgerows, fields and water exists, each one providing different opportunities to feed, to lie up and to breed, and all offering an alternative if one place becomes inadequate for some reason. Only a very adaptable animal could take full advantage of such diversity.

Foxes often lie up in undergrowth or shelter under a farm outbuilding, a garden shed or a fallen tree. They may use crevices in rocky areas, or old drains, or take over part of a badger sett or rabbit warren. They quite often take up residence in buildings – both empty and occupied – but they often dig their own burrows (called earths or dens), especially in dry sandy soils. An earth may have a single entrance but up to four are not unusual. Some large earths may have interconnecting burrows rather than a single tunnel and can have up to a dozen entrances. An earth is marked with a strong and distinctive odour when in use.

▲ *Play fights are vigorous and involve wide open mouths and bared teeth. They rarely last more than a few seconds but are important in teaching young foxes to cope with real aggression when they are older.*

The urban fox

Foxes can be found living in most towns and cities from the Midlands southwards. In northern England and Wales they are scarcer, while in Scotland, both Edinburgh and parts of Glasgow have thriving populations, as do some Irish cities.

They are most likely to be seen in suburban districts built in the 1920s and 1930s, where the houses have sizeable mature gardens. A typical urban fox territory covers between 20 and 40 hectares (50 to 100 acres) of gardens attached to semi-detached houses, and allotments. The smallest territory ever recorded was just 9 hectares (22 acres), in Bristol.

Foxes come out to hunt after dark, preferring gardens that are not too tidy and offer plenty of bushes for shelter. They concentrate on a relatively small area, probably covering only about 0.5 square kilometres (¼ sq mile). They look mostly for scraps – crusts of bread or bacon fat left on a bird table make easy pickings for the urban fox, and a plastic bag of leftovers put out by dustbins may be ripped open for food. They also eat

worms and windfall fruit, but sometimes take pet guinea pigs or rabbits, too. They take no notice of domestic cats.

Urban foxes can sometimes be watched going about their business in the day, seemingly unconcerned by the presence of humans, but generally they

rest while it's light – perhaps on a sun-warmed asphalt roof or a sheltered, hidden patch of grass. During the breeding season, the urban vixen's favourite spot for making a den is the space beneath a garden shed or other outbuilding.

Foxes generally prefer to live above ground and use their dens mainly for breeding, although they tend to take sanctuary in them during wet or cold weather. On warm summer nights they will come out even in the rain because warm, wet conditions are ideal for finding worms at the surface. Most of their activity is at night, but foxes will often emerge in the evenings and even in broad daylight in places where they feel safe.

MIDWINTER CRYING

The male dog fox and female vixen look similar, but males are usually slightly larger and there are minor differences in the shape of the head.

The breeding season lasts from December to February, during which

time the dog fox will remain near to a vixen that is ready to breed, following her closely all the time.

This is the time of year when foxes are most vocal, males calling at night with three or four-note barks, and vixens emitting blood-curdling screams.

The social arrangements of foxes vary according to where they are living. Territory sizes can range from 20 hectares (50 acres) or so in urban areas, to as much as 1600 hectares (4000 acres) in the Scottish hills. Foxes may live alone, in pairs or in family groups. When individuals are old enough to leave the group, how far they go depends on how many foxes are living in the area – the fewer the foxes, the larger each pair's

or group's territory and the farther the foxes will need to disperse. Territories may overlap but only core areas are used frequently. Some parts of a territory may be rarely visited by the territory owners, or used merely to get from one place to another.

Foxes mark territories by squirting urine on to fences, tree trunks and other solid objects at nose height for the information of the next fox that passes by. Faeces also form territorial markers.

Interestingly, marking behaviour is least frequent at territory boundaries but is used right across the area that the fox usually inhabits, and especially along regularly used paths. This means the whole territory is marked, not just its edges.

Catching mice

Mice and voles generally move along narrow runways through grass and other vegetation, where it is hard for the fox to follow. Having located an unwary mouse by the slight noises it makes or by sight, or both, the fox leaps in the air, landing on top of it and using its paws and mouth to trap the prey.

Research has found that dominant individuals leave scent marks no more frequently than subordinates.

LEAVING HOME

When they are about six months old, some of the juveniles begin to move away from the family group. Around three-quarters of male cubs leave their home territory by the time they are a year old, but only about a third of females do so. In large families, the smallest animals are the most likely to leave, either walking non-stop or making a series of short journeys spread over several days or weeks. Few things get in their way in the search for a new home, and foxes have been known to cross rivers and even tidal mudflats. Males go farther than females, sometimes up to 50km (30 miles).

The females that remain in their home area become part of the family group. As many as six additional females may assist with bringing up the cubs of the dominant female in the following year. These 'helpers' guard, groom and play with the young and retrieve them if they stray.

Females are capable of breeding for the first time when they are 10 months old, and their family will then be born around the time of the

◀ *A thick winter coat helps the fox to maintain its body temperature and survive the harshest of weather.*

vixen's own first birthday. However, not all females will breed successfully this early in their lives, and many do not do so until their second year.

ART OF COMMUNICATION

Foxes use a wide variety of facial expressions to convey their moods to each other, just as dogs and people do. Even young cubs do this, making open-mouthed threat gestures towards each other when annoyed.

A variety of body postures indicates either aggressive intent or submission, and foxes also have a great number of calls at their disposal. These vary from the yelping and whining of the cubs to the barks and screams of the adults. One researcher distinguished 40 basic types of sound grouped into 28 different calls.

All this helps the animals to communicate with, and to understand, each other, and to react towards each other in the most appropriate manner.

When provoked, two foxes will rear up on their hind legs and paw at each other, with their mouths wide open, but real aggression is

rare. In autumn and winter, however, as establishing territory and mating become more important, and food becomes increasingly hard to find, fights can be serious. Just occasionally a fox will kill its opponent, but death and serious injuries are infrequent.

HUNTING TECHNIQUES

Strategies vary according to circumstances. Sometimes foxes stalk prey, rushing up to grab it at the last moment. Other times they creep quietly through long grass to pounce on small mammals.

Hunting for earthworms involves trotting rapidly back and forth over areas of short grass on warm moist nights, searching for worms lying on the surface. A keen sense of hearing enables the fox to detect worms by any slight noises they make as they move. Earthworms form a large part of the diet of urban foxes and those living in semi-rural areas, but country foxes eat relatively few of them.

Generally, foxes do not attack or kill many lambs, but often eat dead ones. They eat other carrion as well,

▲ *These fox cubs are eagerly awaiting the return of one of their parents, bringing food back to the den for them to eat or to play with.*

including deer and road kills, biting the feathers off pigeons and other large birds before eating the body.

Foxes raid nesting seabird colonies whenever they get the chance, and in places severely reduce the breeding success of ducks, partridges and pheasants by attacking females that are incubating eggs. They can eat whole clutches and may be responsible for around one third of all pheasant eggs lost to predators.

Occasionally, a fox will kill chickens, or sometimes wild birds, far in excess of the amount needed for food in order to stimulate its attacking instinct. This is called 'surplus killing'. In some gull colonies, more than 200 birds have been killed in a single night. In a chicken coop, the fox may lose control and rush about killing frightened birds for as long as any remain alive. At other times, surplus food may be hidden away – often partially buried – to be retrieved when needed.

CHANGING COAT

From about Easter time, the fox's winter coat moults and the animal can look very moth-eaten, but by midsummer all the old fur has been replaced with a sleek, shorter coat. In autumn, additional hair grows and the thickening of the underfur gives the fox its chunky, almost bushy, winter profile.

NUMBERS GAME

When numbers are high, foxes may suffer from outbreaks of mange, which is caused by scabies mites. Millions of mites build up in the skin, starting at the tail, where hair falls out first. The intense irritation causes constant scratching and the fox sheds its fur. It may lose over half its body weight before dying

Learning through play

Fox cubs are fully weaned at around ten weeks old but they remain dependent on their parents for several more months. They spend the summer playing, but by the time winter arrives young foxes must be ready to fend for themselves.

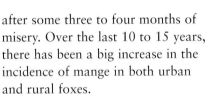 *Cubs learn how to tackle prey by practising on dead animals brought by their parents. At first, though, even picking up a meal can prove to be a challenge.*

after some three to four months of misery. Over the last 10 to 15 years, there has been a big increase in the incidence of mange in both urban and rural foxes.

Male foxes seem to live longer than females, occasionally reaching ten years or more, but around one year is more usual and few survive more than two years. Foxes that leave the area where they were born tend to have a reduced life expectancy, partly because of the hazards that they encounter during their search for a new home. Many die on the roads and it is thought that about 100,000 are killed each year by gamekeepers and others. Foxes often die from poisoning, either through eating illegally set baits, or prey or carrion that has itself been poisoned, sometimes by agricultural chemicals such as insecticides.

Other causes of death include being killed by predators – dogs and birds of prey sometimes kill cubs. Fox hunts (banned in 2005) used to kill about 12,500 a year. Twice that number are destroyed by forestry workers and fox eradication teams. This high mortality rate means that pairs of foxes are unlikely to survive very long and the remaining animal must find a new mate. Despite all this, the fox seems to be holding its own or modestly increasing in numbers.

The wood mouse

Venturing out to feed mostly under cover of darkness, the wood mouse has big eyes that enable it to see well in dense undergrowth and on moonless nights. Acute hearing also helps it to navigate the woodland floor.

Although the wood mouse lives in many habitats, it is most numerous in woodland. Sometimes called the long-tailed field mouse – because it has a very long tail and may live in fields – it also makes its home in gardens and hedges and on arable farmland, where it shelters in dry stone walls.

Wood mice are extremely adaptable creatures that occasionally find their way to urban areas, where they may be one of the few wild mammals present. They are also found in surprisingly open surroundings, such as sand dunes, and even on heather moorland and rocky mountains.

On arable farmland, wood mice from nearby hedges and woods move on to the land afresh each year, to avoid the seasonal harvesting of crops and ploughing of fields. Wood mice in stubble fields leave well-worn paths that are likely to be shared by other small mammals, such as voles.

ALERT AND AGILE

Foraging after darkness has fallen helps wood mice to evade predators. Highly alert creatures, they never stay still for long. Whereas voles and shrews scurry away when frightened, wood mice bound away like tiny kangaroos. They can cover quite a distance at high speed before disappearing down a hole or under a log. They can also climb well.

Despite these advantages, wood mice are often taken by owls and predatory mammals, such as weasels and cats. Their only defence, apart from biting, is a very delicate tail skin. If a predator catches a wood mouse by the tail, the skin comes off so that the animal can escape. However, the skin does not regrow and, after a while, the tail bones drop off. As few wood mice are seen with shortened tails, most presumably either manage to escape unscathed or are killed outright.

The field mouse is fastidiously clean, carefully removing mud from its tail by running it through its paws and using its teeth to scrape off stubborn dirt.

▶ *As the wood mouse moves among the leaves and undergrowth of the woodland floor, it makes soft rustling sounds that may alert predators. Wet weather conditions help the wood mouse to remain undetected because it can travel on damp woodland leaf litter much more quietly than on dry.*

Feeding on fruit

In autumn, the wood mouse often climbs into trees and shrubs to find food, its light weight allowing it to balance on narrow stems. It may use old birds' nests as feeding sites on these forays, leaving them full of the gnawed remains of hawthorn berries or rose hips.

LIFE EXPECTANCY

In winter, the survival of wood mice depends on how much food is available. In times of plenty, more mice live through the cold months so that there are higher numbers in any given area when spring arrives. This can result in springtime aggression between wood mice competing for both food and territories, and many are killed by their own kind.

Large numbers of wood mice also die as a result of entering discarded bottles, perhaps mistaking the neck for a burrow entrance. Others are found drowned in tanks and water containers. Wood mice are vulnerable to poisons used on farms. They often die from consuming large amounts of seeds that have been planted and treated with insecticides to prevent damage by insects. Slug pellets put out to protect farm crops are also known to have a severe effect on wood mouse populations, reducing numbers drastically.

The hazards are such that few adults manage to survive from one year to the next, although in captivity wood mice might occasionally live to be three years old or more. In the wild, their maximum lifespan is 18–20 months. To counteract the shortness of their lives, wood mice reproduce in large numbers.

PROLIFIC BREEDERS

Wood mice generally begin breeding in March. Females may produce as many as nine young in a litter, but usually have between four and seven. The young weigh just 1–2g (a fraction of an ounce) at birth and are born pink, blind and helpless. Their first coat of grey fur begins to appear at about one week of age. At two weeks their teeth start to emerge and their eyes open about three days later. Young born during the summer grow rapidly whereas those born later, between September and October, do less well. Young are usually weaned at 18–22 days, and become independent at less than one month old.

▲ *In woodland, when fresh leaves appear in spring, the wood mouse will feed on them. In autumn and winter it forages at night for seeds and fruit.*

In good conditions, and if the young are born earlier in the year, it may take two months for them to be able to breed. This means they can breed in the same summer they are born, and their mother is also able to breed again that year. Most females have at least two litters in a season, and some may have four before breeding ends, normally in October.

This reproduction rate means that the wood mouse population can increase rapidly. It may result in as many as 40 wood mice living in one hectare (2½ acres) of woodland. In years when trees produce a good seed crop, providing plenty to eat, there can be more than 150 wood mice per hectare (2½ acres). Wood mice numbers fluctuate widely from year to year depending on the weather and availability of food.

OMNIVOROUS DIET

As rodents, wood mice would be expected to eat mainly vegetable material, and they do feed on a wide variety of seeds and green plants. More surprising perhaps is that they also eat a lot of insects, caterpillars and other invertebrates, including worms and small snails, especially in spring and summer. In the autumn, they particularly favour blackberries and other fruits. At this time of year in woodland, they also feed on acorns and the nuts from hazel, beech and other trees.

On farmland, they eat quantities of grain, and may become a nuisance by nibbling the fleshy seeds of cultivated sugar beet, for example.

NESTING IN BURROWS

Wood mice live in burrows, which they often dig for themselves using their forefeet. However, they also make good use of existing burrows, perhaps inherited from a previous

Beech bounty

An opportunistic feeder, the wood mouse tends to eat whatever is available at the time of year. In the autumn, when nuts are plentiful, it may gather an excess so that it can store them for later in the year when food may be scarce.

generation of mice. The cavities left by old, rotted-out tree roots are a useful foundation for a burrow system. Wood mice build their nests within the burrow system, in winter constructing them in deeper tunnels than in warmer weather. They line the nest with grass, moss or dry leaves.

Some wood mice nest above ground, using a woodpecker hole or other tree cavity. They may occupy nestboxes intended for birds or dormice, especially during the late summer and early autumn. For their bedding, they collect dead leaves from the ground and carry them up the tree to the nestbox.

This habit distinguishes a wood mouse nest from a dormouse nest. Dormice gather leaves from the tree canopy to line their nests, which are made of shredded honeysuckle bark. Birds that use nestboxes – mainly tits – build their nests with moss and a lot of animal hair and feathers, whereas wood mice seldom use such materials.

▶ *A wood mouse is able to move with great agility in woods and hedgerows. It can leap 2m (6½ft) from branch to branch and can jump nearly 1m (3ft) up from the ground.*

TERRITORIAL AGGRESSION

Due to the small size of the wood mouse and its nocturnal life, which largely takes place under cover or below ground, little is known about its behaviour in the wild. In captivity, wood mice – especially breeding males – can be aggressive, and it is likely that aggression also plays a significant role in the lives of wild wood mice.

They live mostly solitary lives and usually avoid meeting dominant individuals, at least in the summer. Females generally have their own territories, but males occupy larger areas, overlapping with those used by other males and several females. In sand dunes, for example, some males may occupy areas of more than 36,000 square metres (387,500 sq ft).

Wood mice travel long distances for such a small mammal, sometimes venturing more than 2km (1 mile) from their nest in a night.

WINTER TORPOR

Any aggressive tendencies are put on hold for the winter. Wood mice do not defend territories then, but instead may live together in small groups. This is particularly likely among young mice, perhaps from the same family.

It is difficult for small animals to generate the energy they need to stay sufficiently warm in winter. In cold or freezing weather conditions, especially if there is a shortage of food, wood mice may reduce their body temperature during the day. They become cold to the touch, saving the energy expended in remaining fully warm blooded. These torpid mice are not hibernating – wood mice do not hibernate – and wake up to resume normal activity at night.

The fallow deer

Despite being shy and easily startled, the fallow deer often ventures out of its woodland shelter into parks, fields and other grassy spaces to graze in large herds, the fawns trotting after their mothers.

The Normans introduced the fallow deer to this country nearly a thousand years ago, specifically so that it could be hunted, and it is now the most widespread deer in the British Isles.

Typically, fallow deer are a rich brown with a black stripe down the middle of the back and large white spots on the body – the pattern of spots is unique to each animal. In winter, the general coat colour turns a paler, duller greyish brown, and the spots become less distinct. This winter colour may be the origin of

▶ *Not surprisingly for an animal that was long hunted, fallow deer are nervous animals. They have excellent eyesight and hearing, and an acute sense of smell. Their large ears, which measure more than half the length of the head, are mobile and turn quickly towards any small sound.*

Challenging males

During the autumn rut bucks, resplendent in new antlers, compete for mating rights over does. A challenger struts alongside a posturing buck until the weaker gives way, or they fight by clashing antlers. These encounters do not always end in a fight and body language plays a major part in settling many disputes.

the deer's name – 'fealou' is an old English word for pale brown. Several colour variations exist – the most common is 'menil'. Menil deer are very pale and their white spots are large and conspicuous. The overall result closely resembles the classic Disney cartoon image of 'Bambi'.

FLAT ANTLERS

Male fallow deer, called bucks, are the only deer in Britain to grow flattened antlers. These are usually described as 'palmate', because the shape resembles the palm of a hand – flat with short finger-like prongs at the edges. They are shed between April and June and regrow over the summer in preparation for the rut,

or breeding season. During the regrowth, antlers are covered in 'velvet', a soft furry covering of skin that makes the antler look thick and blunt. This is scraped off on tree trunks and branches in late summer, leaving the bony interiors exposed. Each year, the new set of antlers grows bigger than the last – in mature bucks they can be up to 70cm (28in) long.

HERD INSTINCT

A sociable species, fallow deer are usually found in single-sex herds of up to 50 or more. Bucks move to join the females, or does, and their young in about September. Older bucks may return to the same place they rutted

▲ *Although rival males will usually attempt to solve disputes by display, fights are not uncommon in the rut. The antagonists lock antlers and wrestle, but these contests are usually more a test of strength than a genuine attempt to do each other harm.*

in previous years, and mature does also frequently revisit familiar areas to breed. Sometimes does are accompanied by their daughters and granddaughters, and bucks may interbreed with their own offspring.

Most does over 16 months old breed every year. However, when the population density is especially high, there is often insufficient food to support the whole herd.

Many animals are less well fed and, as a result, a high proportion of females may fail to breed. In this way, a natural form of population control operates among the deer.

Typically, each buck will vigorously defend his own patch and attempt to keep a harem of females to himself, although sometimes two bucks may work together to defend a harem. During the rut, the bucks are very active and noisy – they will strut about and perhaps clash antlers with a persistent rival. The does may ignore these displaying males but the bucks still nuzzle them frequently and make groaning noises.

All of this behaviour may be seen in deer parks, but is harder to observe in the countryside.

◄ A fawn keeps very still, waiting for its mother's return. The doe may continue to provide it with milk for up to nine months, by which time the young deer will be almost fully mature.

▼ Fallow deer tend to stay close to well-established woodlands, although they may venture into the open to graze.

WOBBLY START

After the rut, the bucks often disperse to live separately from the does once again, while the following summer the doe gives birth to her fawn. Usually she produces just one but very occasionally there are twins. Fawns are generally born in June but sometimes may appear a little later in the summer. On average, a fawn weighs about 4½kg (10lb) at birth.

Fawns are born among clumps of bracken, long grass or other cover. As soon as possible, the mother moves some distance away in order to avoid drawing attention to her offspring, although she returns at intervals to suckle it. The fawn lies quietly with its neck stretched out along the ground or folded back against the flank.

For the first few hours, which may sometimes extend to days, the fawn reacts to danger by 'freezing' – remaining motionless and relying on its spotted camouflage to avoid detection. But fawns are surprisingly agile, even when only a few hours old, and their response to danger soon becomes a swift retreat. After

about a week, the fawn joins its mother and becomes part of a social group, following the herd and learning to feed itself.

GRASS EATERS

Fallow deer are creatures of habit and will use the same tracks and paths repeatedly to get from place to place. Each animal is probably familiar with an area of about 20 hectares (50 acres) or more. They are woodland animals, preferring deciduous trees to conifers and plantations, but this environment is used mainly for shelter, so they can live happily in quite small copses.

Unlike other deer, they prefer to feed by grazing grass rather than browsing leaves off trees. About 60 per cent of their summer diet is grass. In the autumn, they eat acorns if these are available, together with fallen fruits. Over winter they turn to heather, conifer needles, brambles, ivy and other such vegetation, but they prefer grass whenever they can find it. Even at this time, when the grass is not growing, it still forms about a fifth of their food intake.

The red squirrel

Fast and agile, the red squirrel spends most of its life in trees, leaping from branch to branch in search of pine cones and nuts. Thanks to vast tracts of pine forest, Scotland has become the red squirrel's stronghold.

Once known as the 'common squirrel' the red squirrel lived in most parts of Britain until as recently as 60 years ago. Today, it has disappeared from most of England and Wales, although it is still found throughout much of Scotland, on some offshore islands and in Ireland.

The British winter has been considered a factor in its decline. This may seem unlikely considering that the animals survive successfully in Scandinavia and eastern Europe, where winters are much colder. However, they are also drier and it is possible that in mild and damp conditions red squirrels are less resistant to disease. In the past, disease is known to have reduced red squirrel numbers substantially – even before the arrival of the grey squirrel.

COMPETING FOR FOOD

The grey squirrel was introduced to several places in Britain from America around the turn of the 19th century and has now replaced the red squirrel in many of the red's previous territories. It is often thought that the grey squirrel ousted the red because it is bigger and therefore competes aggressively for food, but the reasons for the grey's ascendancy are more complex than that.

▶ *Special 'double jointed' ankles allow the red squirrel to hang by its feet or even run down a tree head first. The animal uses its strong, sharp claws to grip the bark, often leaving scars on the tree trunk.*

Conditions in Britain were never ideal for the red squirrel. Not only is the weather unsuitable, but the woodland has always been mainly deciduous with a lack of mature conifer forests, where the red squirrel prefers to live. However, the red squirrel was able to cope before the introduction of the grey squirrel because it can live in places where a mix of different types of trees offers a range of food, which it identifies by smell. The red squirrel eats various nuts, berries, buds and insects, as well as the pine seeds that form the main part of its diet. It gnaws the scales from pine cones to find the seeds.

While red and grey squirrels seem able to exist together for a while, once the reds decline they are unable to recover their numbers. On average, once the grey squirrel arrives in an area, the red squirrel disappears from it within 15 years. Pine cones are rarely plentiful in mixed woodland, which can usually support twice as many grey squirrels as red ones. The larger number of grey squirrels means that they eat more of the available food, such as hazelnuts. This leaves fewer nuts for the red squirrels, forcing them to eat less nourishing foods, such as fungi. The main autumn food crop in most of Britain's lowland woods is acorns, which red squirrels – unlike greys – cannot digest. This makes it more difficult

for red squirrels to fatten up sufficiently in preparation for winter. Scotland, which has more extensive areas of pine forest and fewer oak woodlands, offers better feeding opportunities for red squirrels.

NEW FORESTRY

Nevertheless, the planting of extensive conifer plantations in recent years has not assisted red squirrels as much as might have been expected. Often the conifers grown in these plantations do not provide cone crops that are as abundant as the native Scots pine produces. Plantation conifers are normally harvested at about 30 years old, which is too young for them to have produced mature cones. The trees tend to be

▲ *A red squirrel may occasionally come down from the trees to drink, especially in dry weather, but on the ground, it is vulnerable to predators such as wildcats and foxes.*

planted so densely and on such poor soils that they bear few cones and the seeds they bear are of little nutritional value.

In the 1960s, public outcry about the scenic impact of big conifer plantations resulted in the planting of broad screens of nut-bearing deciduous trees, such as beech and oaks. Now that these trees are producing plenty of nuts, grey squirrels are spreading rapidly into former red squirrel strongholds, such as Thetford Chase in East Anglia.

Bounding gait

On its few forays to the ground, a red squirrel usually either keeps completely still or moves at high speed. It runs in a series of bounds, its long, strong hind legs and light weight making fast acceleration possible.

In British woodlands, a phenomenon called 'mast years', possibly triggered by a time of drought, occurs when trees such as oak, beech and chestnut produce massive autumn crops of nuts. In other years there may be almost no nuts at all. As the red squirrel spends the majority of its time foraging in tree tops, gathering only a small percentage of its food from the woodland floor, it is soon in danger of starvation when the nut crop is poor.

High winds, heavy rain or deep snow make it difficult for squirrels to forage and, although the red squirrel does not hibernate, it is less active in bad weather. Its streamlined body shape allows it to climb with great agility among the highest branches, especially on the thin twigs that bear the flowers, buds, pollen, seeds, nuts and cones on which it feeds, but its low fat reserves make survival more difficult during long periods of bad weather. At those times, it prefers to remain in its nest, known as a drey, concealed in the shelter of the tree canopy. The squirrel must eventually venture out to look for food because it cannot go for more than a few days without eating. Then it may need to

▲ *Its flexible body and powerful hind legs allow the red squirrel to take a flying leap between trees. Not only agile, the red squirrel is also robust and often takes risks.*

forage during all the daylight hours, on the ground as well as in the tree tops. Red squirrel sightings often take place in winter – in summer, it is seen less often because it is mostly active early in the morning, and rests in the middle of the day.

Red squirrels usually live for about three years. Poor autumn harvests and challenging weather conditions are

Burying nuts

The squirrel pushes a nut into soft earth, then repeatedly stamps on the ground covering it with both front paws. When the nut is firmly hidden, the squirrel springs away, tail held high, to search for another nut to store against harder times.

greater dangers than predators, few of which are able to catch the athletic red squirrel in the trees. However, the young in particular are occasionally killed by predatory mammals on the ground. Red squirrels are also sometimes killed by traffic when attempting to cross roads.

Building roads through forests slices them into smaller patches, while open farmland or sprawling urban developments may isolate areas of forestry. Since red squirrels feed mainly in the tree canopy, they need continuous woodland to be able to climb from tree to tree. If a forest becomes fragmented, squirrels, unable to find enough to eat in small copses and prevented from travelling to new areas, will decline in numbers.

PREPARING FOR WINTER

In autumn, red squirrels are particularly active as they search for food, such as beech mast, to store for winter. They also eat heartily at this time of year. In years when tree seeds are less abundant, the squirrels start the winter in poor condition and may die from starvation or from disease. The survivors are undernourished and their young often perish. Females that are fit and reasonably fat at the start of winter are more likely to breed successfully the following spring, producing more milk to nourish their young.

SPRING BREEDING

Red squirrels often begin courtship on warm days in January, with the mating season lasting until March. It can take the male some time to court the female, and the pair play chasing games along the branches. Females may have several mates each year. Young arrive between March and April, and there may be a second breeding period, with young produced from July to August. In southern England young may be born as early as January and as late as September.

Males take no part in rearing the young, which are born in the drey. Constructed from twigs, the drey is about 30cm (12in) across and usually wedged securely against a tree trunk or built in a hole in a tree. The young are born blind, naked and helpless. If the nest is disturbed, the female carries each one in her mouth to a new nest nearby. By three weeks old, the young have fur and they open their eyes at four weeks. They leave the nest when they are about two months old, soon becoming independent of their mother and growing the distinctive bright chestnut summer coat of the adult.

▼ *Holding its food in its forepaws, the red squirrel gnaws it with its sharp teeth. It may be attracted into gardens by bird tables or bird feeders hanging in trees.*

The pipistrelle

This tiny bat is mostly seen at dusk, often in open woodland, when it emerges from its roost and begins to feed. Fantastically manoeuvrable, it is able to snatch its insect prey out of the air while flying at high speed.

With a wingspan of around 20cm (8in) and a typical weight of less than 8g (¼oz) – barely more than a lump of sugar – the pipistrelle is Britain's smallest bat. Contrary to popular belief, not all small bats are pipistrelles, although it may be impossible to distinguish them as they flit by in the gathering dark.

Until very recently, most pipistrelles in Britain were thought to be one species, the so-called common pipistrelle. But new technology, in the form of ultrasound recorders, has revealed that there are in fact two different species co-existing throughout Britain and Ireland. First identified by a difference in frequency of their echo-location calls, they are now known as the 45 pipistrelle – *Pipistrellus pipistrellus*, calling at 45 kilohertz (kHz) – and the 55 pipistrelle (*Pipistrellus pygmaeus*, calling at 55 kHz). Researchers soon found tiny physical differences between the two species – 55 pipistrelles are slightly smaller and paler, while 45 pipistrelles have a dark 'mask' around their eyes.

SMALL SPACES

Of all bats, pipistrelles are the ones most often associated with buildings, entering them in search of suitable temperature conditions. The females need warm places to rear their young and frequently invade buildings in considerable numbers in May or June. The males need cooler places

▲ *Unlike birds' sturdy feathered wings, bats' wings are almost translucent. They are made from modified hand bones, with a thin membrane of skin stretched between each 'finger'.*

and usually remain alone or in small groups. While bats are usually associated with deserted places such as derelict buildings, pipistrelles are just as likely to be found in modern bungalows. They can get into very small crevices, through gaps less than 1cm (½in) across, and they especially like to squeeze up behind the weather boarding and hanging tiles that clad the walls of many cottages and houses. They are common in old churches, but are more likely to be found behind noticeboards or in gaps between beams and walls than flying around the belfry. The church bells would cause great distress to creatures with such sensitive hearing.

Pipistrelles are at home flying over gardens and parks, including those in towns and large cities. They also occur in other habitats, such as farmland and open woodland, and are most abundant near water, where insects are plentiful. They like to fly along linear features such as rivers, tree lines and hedges, which are easy to follow in the dark, and help the bats to orientate themselves. This is important because they may forage an area up to 3km (1¾ miles) from their roosts – a long way for a creature that is only 4cm (1½in) or so long.

PREDATORS ON PATROL

Pipistrelles emerge from their daytime roosts soon after sunset, earlier on warm nights. They feed at night by flying fast, between 2 and 20 metres (7–70ft) above the ground, in search of small flying insects. To hunt their prey, pipistrelles rely entirely on echolocation – a natural form of radar based on high-frequency sound inaudible to humans. They patrol one 'beat' for a few minutes, then zoom off to another, perhaps returning to the first area later. If there are few insects to be found they are likely to give up on the area quickly and try somewhere else, but when there is plenty of food they may continue to fly around the same patch for two hours or more.

Their main prey are midges and slow-flying insects such as caddis flies, but their diet varies according to what is most abundant on the night. Warm, still nights are best and feeding intensity is greatest at dusk

▶ Occasionally pipistrelles may catch larger insects such as moths. These cannot be dealt with in mid-air, and are usually carried to a perch to be dismembered and eaten.

How many are there?

By mapping the distribution of nursery roosts over a wide area, it is possible roughly to estimate the population density of bats. In the case of pipistrelles, researchers in Scotland have found an average density of about five breeding females per square kilometre (13 per square mile). Assuming that there are equal numbers of males and females in the population, this would add up to about two million pipistrelles in Britain. However, it is hard to find all the roosts in a given area, and some areas may provide much better habitat than others. Densities may be higher than estimated and the total population could be somewhat larger.

Conversely, counts during the 1970s and 1980s suggest that this species has declined in numbers, perhaps by more than half in places. In the 1960s, it was not unusual to find colonies of more than 1000 pipistrelles, but by 1987 there were very few such colonies left.

when the bats are hungry after their day's rest. They can catch up to 20 insects per minute and may consume several hundred in a night.

MATING AND BREEDING

Pipistrelles live in colonial groups throughout the year and it is very rare for them to leave their home colony to go to live with another group. During the winter, mixed-sex groups are formed and the bats mate – then around Easter, the females fly off to form nursery roosts. These maternity groups average about 40 to 60 bats, but there may occasionally be several hundred present. Because babies are born hairless, it is essential that the females find a warm place in which to rear their young, as they do not make nests or insulate the roost in any way.

Females can breed in their first year, and usually produce just one baby a year. A baby bat is nearly one-third the size of its mother.

Night hunter

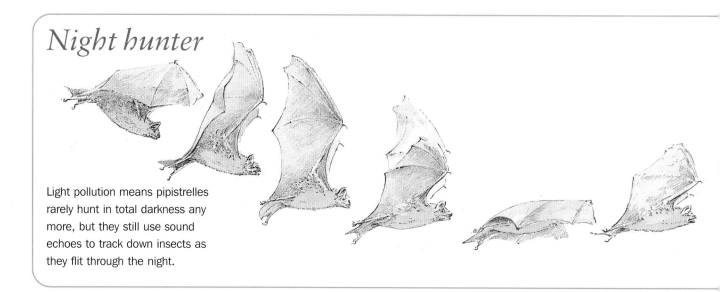

Light pollution means pipistrelles rarely hunt in total darkness any more, but they still use sound echoes to track down insects as they flit through the night.

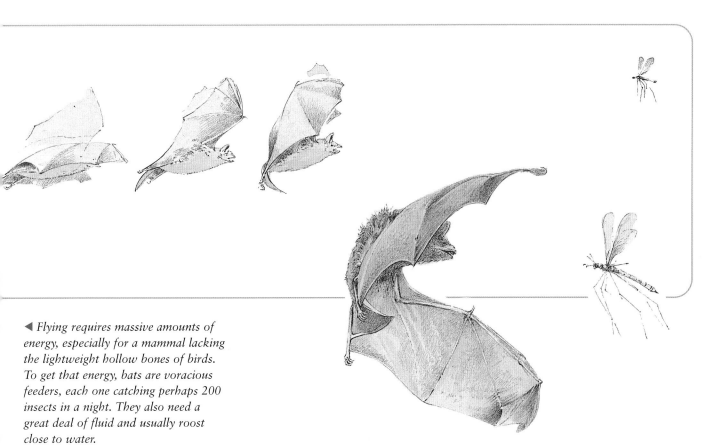

◀ *Flying requires massive amounts of energy, especially for a mammal lacking the lightweight hollow bones of birds. To get that energy, bats are voracious feeders, each one catching perhaps 200 insects in a night. They also need a great deal of fluid and usually roost close to water.*

This is equivalent to a human baby weighing about 18kg (40lb), so twins are rare. The foetus develops over a period of about six weeks, and birth usually takes place in late June or early July. Babies grow quickly, nourished by their mother's milk; she returns to the roost in the night to provide additional feeds.

FIRST MONTHS

By about three weeks, the babies are furry, their eyes are open, and they begin to fly. Most of the females will have offspring by then, and adults and young all flit around the roost entrance in the evening. July is when householders are most likely to notice a nursery roost, but soon after the babies can fly, the whole group leaves of its own accord, and will not return until the following summer.

In periods of cold weather, when the mother bats have not fed well, their hungry babies may crawl out of the roost before they can fly properly. Even in good years, when the young first leave the roost they cannot fly well and often fall to the ground. Here they may be caught by cats or found by people. They can be rescued, fed, and released, but caring for bats is a painstaking job and they do not respond well to extended captivity. Sometimes bad weather coincides with the main period for raising young, and mortality rates can be very high. This is serious because offspring cannot be replaced for a full year. However, if the babies make it through the first few months, pipistrelles enjoy a fairly high survival rate, with almost two-thirds living from one year to the next.

PEST CONTROL

Bats generally cause little damage to property, and they very rarely spread disease – in this country at least. If large colonies return to the same place year after year, accumulated droppings may become a little smelly if they get damp. In churches there may be a few droppings on the pews. However, any problems that bats may cause are trivial compared to the benefits they provide. For instance, many of the insects they eat are a nuisance, such as midges and mosquitoes, or damaging to houses, such as woodworm beetles.

Rare species

A third pipistrelle bat, previously thought to be a mere visitor from the Continent, is now known to be resident in Britain. This is Nathusius' pipistrelle (*Pipistrellus nathusii*), first recorded here in 1969. It has been found all around the country, from Kent to Shetland, and even on North Sea oil rigs. Larger than the common pipistrelle it is otherwise similar, except for small differences in its teeth. Kuhl's pipistrelle (*Pipistrellus kuhli*) has also been recorded in Britain, but only once.

The red deer

With the arrival of warmer weather, red deer move on to upland slopes, seeking fresh grass as well as new growth on trees and shrubs. Unlike some deer, they are both grazers and browsers and thrive on whatever food is available.

Ever since the ice retreated at the end of the last Ice Age, red deer have inhabited the forests and uplands of Britain. Once common, the population declined as the forests were systematically cleared for fuel and to make way for farmland and eventually housing, but recently this trend has been reversed. New forests of conifers have been planted, especially in Scotland, and the red deer is now more numerous than it has been for centuries.

INCREASING NUMBERS

The total British wild deer population probably exceeds 360,000. Around 95 per cent are in Scotland with a handful in Wales, and the rest scattered in various parts of England including Cumbria, the Pennines, the Peak District, East Anglia and parts of the south-west. In Ireland, where it is uncertain whether the species is native or was introduced, about 800 red deer live in Killarney National Park in the south-west. On the other side of the country in Wicklow National Park, an introduced relative – the sika deer – has interbred with the red deer so extensively that no purebred red deer are left. Approximately 70,000 red deer are farmed in Britain and Ireland and 7500 or so are kept in deer parks, where they can be watched at fairly close quarters.

▶ *In deer parks, grazing by red deer results in trees developing a distinctive 'browse line'. Leaves survive only above the height that the deer can reach.*

Red deer are essentially forest animals but they are highly adaptable and thrive on moorland and in upland hill country. Where food and cover are in good supply, densities can often exceed 15 per square kilometre (under half a square mile).

FEEDING HABITS

Red deer are active throughout both day and night, resting and taking short naps when they can. Their days are divided by between five and nine feeding cycles. Red deer are ruminants, so after eating they lie up somewhere safe to chew the cud. This is an effective way of digesting leaves and grass whereby the food is regurgitated and chewed for a second time. Once the process is complete, the deer venture out to feed again. This routine ensures that they spend just a short time in the open before returning to the safety of tree cover.

Safety in numbers

Fresh new leaves are an irresistible temptation to these one-year old hinds. Deer tend to feed in groups, not only because the best food might be concentrated in one area, but also as a safety precaution. The more deer in a herd, the better the chances that any approaching danger will be detected. Hinds generally gather into herds with their offspring and non-breeding males.

DEER CULLS

In deer parks, grazing by deer can cause damage to trees. The deer like to nibble at the leaves and young trees need to be protected from them.

In the wild, the deer are not confined so do not attack all the trees so voraciously. Nevertheless, they do have a serious impact, especially on native pine forests and young conifer plantations. Unless the deer are fenced out, which is expensive, they will nibble the young trees and stunt their growth. Sometimes a tree crop is ruined or the trees grow in distorted shapes. For this reason, deer are often culled by foresters. On major Scottish estates, deer stalking has been developed as a source of income over the last 150 years.

In parks, the deer are also culled each year to maintain a constant population. This entails shooting about 15 per cent of the animals. Without management, the deer quickly become too numerous for the park to support and many would starve during the winter when there is insufficient food available for them all. Red deer do sometimes starve in hill country where the food supply is poor. Up to 65 per cent of calves may die during their first winter, especially towards the end, before new plant growth has begun. If the weather is intensely cold, or if prolonged snow cover prevents access to food, the mortality rate will rise steeply. Adults are less affected, but older individuals with worn teeth may not be able to process their food properly and this reduces their chances of survival.

Antler growth

When male red deer are a few months old, their antlers begin to grow. Each year in the spring – from mid-March to the end of April – the antlers are shed and replaced by a new set, bigger than the previous year's with the addition of an extra prong, called a tine, and covered by a fine furry skin called 'velvet'. The older stags shed their antlers first, and the number of tines does not always correspond exactly to the animal's age.

By the time the antlers reach their full size they are no longer encased in velvet, and the stags are ready for the rut.

Ready for the rut

The whole point of the ritualised performance of rutting is to ensure that the maximum proportion of the population is fathered by the strongest males.

The top stags pay a high price. Once the rut begins, they cannot afford to rest or take time off for feeding. A lapse in attention by a breeding stag may allow any of his rivals to sneak in and steal one or more of his hinds. Mating can occur at any time of the day or night, so constant vigilance is necessary.

The stags need to keep bellowing out their challenge and call to females, as well as patrol the group to stop them straying. They also need to maintain their dark coat and the heavy aroma that accompanies them by wallowing in mud and urine.

After a few weeks of such activity, the stags are pretty well worn out and may have lost over 20 per cent of their body weight. For this reason, the biggest stags stop rutting first, but by that time they will have mated with almost all the females in the harem, so even if a younger animal then takes over the herd, he will father few or no calves since the hinds are already pregnant.

Most active stags will father about two dozen young in their lifetime, but their life span is likely to be shorter than that of the females, largely because of the stresses of the rut.

Displaying stags

For male red deer in the rutting season, the display of social status is all important. The angle of the head, held high, and thickness of neck are important in the body language of rutting red deer stags, as they gauge each other's power and strength.

▶ *A single calf is the norm. Rarely, twins may be born where there is a plentiful supply of food, such as in a deer park.*

MATING RIVALRY

The ritual of red deer stags attracting hinds (females) is the culmination of the deer's annual life cycle.

The rut, as the mating season is called, begins in late September and peaks in mid-October. The stags move to the same area they have used in previous years and each one attempts to gather as many hinds as possible by roaring loudly and actively herding the females. They compete to mate with as many hinds as possible and success depends upon establishing social status.

SOCIAL CLIMBERS

A deer's place in the social hierarchy is settled by the exhibition of various status symbols, notably the antlers. If possible, a stag will avoid using his antlers as weapons since a fight with a rival involves the risk of serious injury or death. So the animals attempt to bluff each other into admitting defeat. A stag will parade up and down, showing off his antlers, thick neck and dark colour. Other stags, particularly younger ones with smaller antlers, will often not even attempt a challenge. An older, more confident animal might indulge in 'parallel walking', marching up and down alongside a dominant stag to see if he will give way. Each eyes the other and only when neither will back down does a physical tussle take place, with antlers locked together and each animal straining to throw the other off balance. Finally, one will concede defeat, leaving the other in sole possession of the harem.

The hinds will be attracted to the stags that display the highest status, that is the ones that roar loudest and most often, and have the biggest antlers. Occasionally, an impressive stag may attract as many as 50 hinds.

Stags do not usually begin to rut until their fifth or sixth year. They may wander for several years before settling down in an area of around 200–400 hectares (500–1000 acres), returning each September to the place where they were first successful in attracting a harem. Typically, a stag may have three or four years of breeding. Hinds are less adventurous and tend to remain close to their birth place, moving around with the seasons as food becomes available.

FIT TO BREED

Where food is plentiful, in deer parks for example, the hinds can breed in the year following their birth.

Where food is poor, breeding may be delayed for another year, possibly two. Similarly, while most hinds will breed every year, they will not do so if they are in poor condition, and on open upland it is usual for a third of the females not to breed in any one year.

Pregnancy lasts around 250 days and usually results in the birth of a single calf although very occasionally, in forested areas with a good food

◄ *Red deer are adaptable animals. They prefer good-quality grass, but will feed on leaves, shoots and any other available vegetation.*

▼ *Outside the breeding season, males are usually quite at ease with each other and often form male herds.*

supply – or in deer parks – twins may be born. However, losses are high, especially in hill country, where a female may manage to raise only four offspring in her entire lifetime of around ten years.

CALF LIFE

The young are mostly born between late May and mid-June, with each hind retreating to a secluded spot to give birth alone. The mother has to double her intake of food in the early days to ensure her calf's rapid growth. She may need to wander up to a kilometre (over half a mile) away from the calf's hiding place to obtain the food necessary to keep up a good supply of milk – but she returns to feed her calf every two or three hours in the first few days. After that, the

frequency of suckling gradually decreases, although the calf may suckle for up to seven months. The hind identifies her calf by scent.

The calf is born fully furred with its eyes open and it can run surprisingly fast even when only a few hours old. If threatened, though, a calf stays absolutely still, relying on the camouflage of its white-spotted brown coat to protect it. In the past, wolves were their main predator but wolves are now extinct in the British Isles. Occasionally, golden eagles are known to take very young calves.

After about a week, the calves join their mothers to form a herd, often with the young gathered together in a 'creche' where they spend their time leaping and playing among themselves.

The mountain hare

On the high moors, a brown hare with white legs lopes through the spring heather in the evening light, stopping occasionally to nibble at new young shoots, and pausing from time to time to get a better view of its surroundings.

During the last Ice Age, mountain hares lived all over the British Isles, but during the following 10,000 years the improving climate forced the hares to retreat to the colder uplands and they gradually died out over much of the country, except the Highlands of Scotland and Ireland.

However, during the 19th century, mountain hares were reintroduced into parts of England, Scotland and Wales, with varying degrees of success. In 1885, for example, mountain hares were introduced to the Vaynol estate near Bangor in North Wales, and by the turn of the century they had become numerous in the mountains of Snowdonia. Hares are now extinct in those regions, but both the date and the cause of the decline remain unclear. It seems likely that humans, climatic conditions and competition from sheep were all contributory factors.

In the Pennines, present-day mountain hares are derived from introductions in 1850 and 1870, with more being released in Yorkshire near Greenfield between 1880 and 1882. The animals spread until they were common around Sheffield and could be found through Derbyshire to the Goyt Valley moors of Cheshire by the turn of the century. Mountain hares

were also released in the Cheviots and the Lake District but these did not survive.

In England, mountain hares are now spread over about 250 square kilometres (97 square miles), including parts of the Peak District National Park, especially in areas with well managed heather moors. Since the Peak District is popular with tourists and hill walkers, the hares have to live with a high level of disturbance from humans.

Sheep are also abundant and compete with the hares for food. Despite these problems, the isolated Pennine population survives and although it fluctuates, plummeting in years with especially cool, damp summers to a small percentage (perhaps as low as 4 per cent) of its peak numbers, it benefits from the conservation measures that have been put in place to protect scarce breeding birds in the Peak National Park.

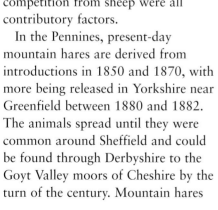

▶ *The hare uses its highly attuned sense of hearing to listen for any predators, such as foxes and stoats, that may be approaching.*

SCOTLAND AND IRELAND

Mountain hares have fared better in the uplands of Scotland and in Ireland, where they are native animals, having survived when those in the rest of the country disappeared. However, the mountain hares found on the Scottish islands are not native. They were introduced to Mull, Skye, Raasay, mainland Shetland, the Outer Hebrides, Scalpay, Jura and the Orkneys, and flourished for a while, but their long-term survival has been poor. Nevertheless, the mountain hare seems secure in Scotland, particularly on heather moorland managed for grouse. The hares average about 10–20 per square kilometre (25–50 per square mile) but in some exceptionally favourable habitats there are 20 times as many.

▲ *During the transition from winter to summer coat, the mountain hare has white legs and feet with a brown body. The hare can run at speeds of up to 64km/h (40mph).*

Winter white

Between October and January, mountain hares in Scotland and England shed their brown summer coats and grow pure white fur. The change of colour is triggered by fluctuations in the levels of a hormone that stimulates the production of the pigment known as melanin. These hormone levels are influenced by light levels and day length. One advantage of the white coat is that white radiates less body heat than a darker coat.

However, it is normally assumed that the pale coat provides protection from predators in winter by camouflaging the hare against white snow.

In fact, British mountains often have little snow and white hares are then very conspicuous, standing out clearly against the dark heather and peat. Under such circumstances, a white coat is clearly more of a liability than an asset. The winter whiteness is an adaptation more appropriate to the hare's original Arctic home, where snow is guaranteed and persistent. It is less suited to the warmer climate of Britain.

The hares do show some flexibility, though, losing their white coat sooner in warm spring weather and growing it earlier at higher altitudes than lower down. In the relatively mild climate of Ireland, the hares are brown all the year round but the ears, feet and tail turn white in winter.

Good grooming habits

In winter hares often sit in fairly prominent places on open ground. On a rare sunny day in the Scottish Highlands, it may be possible to watch a hare take advantage of the warm sunshine and spend a few minutes grooming its fur.

All animals living at higher altitudes face the problem of low temperatures, particularly during clear, frosty nights. The mountain hare is adapted to its habitat with thick, fluffy fur, but its coat must be kept in good condition to ensure maximum heat insulation. Grooming takes place at least once a day.

Hares groom themselves by licking with their tongues and using their teeth as a comb. The hind feet of the mountain hare are fringed with long stiff hairs. This extra fur keeps the feet warm and spreads the animal's weight to prevent it from sinking into soft snow. The feet often pick up dirt and the hare may spend several minutes raking through the fur with its teeth, spreading out the toes so that it can work down between each one.

The strong hind feet are useful for reaching behind the ears to scratch an itch or for cleaning purposes. In fact, the hind legs are long enough to clean almost every part of the body, after the paw has been licked. Parts of the rump are groomed using the forefeet.

When grooming one of its ears, the hare pulls it down with a front paw and then combs it with the 'thumb' claw high up on the foot. Finally, the hare licks its paws and begins to wash its face in a similar way to a cat – sitting upright and licking each front paw in turn before rubbing it carefully over its head and face. Hares rarely carry fleas, although they do pick up sheep ticks.

In harsh mountainous areas of western Scotland, there are on average fewer than two mountain hares per square kilometre (fewer than five per square mile). Fewer still are found on the low moors, and this animal is generally absent from farmland. The total number of mountain hares in Scotland is around 350,000, divided among about six separate populations.

In Ireland, by contrast, mountain hares are generally more numerous and have adapted to live in lowland as well as upland regions. Brown hares, on the other hand, have been brought over from Britain many times, but only a few still survive.

◄ Tufts of fur on the hare's broad hind feet provide insulation from the cold snow. They leave typically wide footprints, while the front feet leave small, round prints.

FORAGING FOR FOOD

Mountain hares occupy home territories of about 50–100 hectares (125–250 acres), but they do not always use the whole of this space. They tend to have a daytime resting place high upon the hillside, and travel a kilometre (half a mile) or more each evening to feed at a lower altitude. They use regular routes, which develop into distinct trails across the moors.

When there has been a fall of snow they may have to feed in a different place each night, depending on where the snow has drifted to reveal vegetation. Dry powdery snow is normally blown away allowing hares to feed, but in Britain the snow often forms slushy blankets that can take many weeks to melt. During the long winter of 1963, for example, extensive areas of long-lasting wet snow resulted in the death of many mountain hares in the Peak District.

Lower and sheltered areas may be completely blanketed, so the hares have to be quite flexible in their feeding behaviour, especially when snowfalls restrict access to food at the beginning of the breeding season. In summer, mountain hares may move to higher ground and establish a new territory, perhaps over 300m (1000ft) higher than their winter range.

SURVIVAL RATES

Like their close relative the brown hare, but unlike their other British relative the rabbit, mountain hares do not dig burrows or build a nest. Instead, they make a 'form' in long heather, with the stems bitten off to create a sheltered space. Here the hare is protected from the wind and is almost completely hidden from predators. Individuals do not share their form with others, although they may sometimes feed together

◀ Young mountain hares resemble rabbits, but do not have an orange patch on the nape of the neck, and they share the black ear tips of the brown hare. They are best identified by the setting – mountain hares are rarely seen in the lowlands, except in Ireland.

female, so the mountain hare does at least have the potential for rapid population recovery, given favourable conditions.

ARCTIC LIVING

The mountain hare is adapted to living in the harsh conditions found in the Arctic. It copes easily with the cold, dry weather normally experienced over most of its range, but in Britain it encounters a more humid environment. Wet summers are particularly prevalent in Britain's maritime climate and can cause significant problems for mountain hares. Wet heather and grass tussocks shed water on to the hares as they move about, reducing the insulation provided by their fine fur. As a result, young leverets, in particular, can lose body heat very quickly.

Mountain hares do not travel far outside their home territories, usually just a few kilometres. This means that if hares are lost from one area, they are unlikely to return.

in groups. Aggression between males sometimes occurs, but the females are more tolerant of each other.

Mountain hares produce up to three litters per year, and in each litter there may be between one and four young. The leverets are born between March and early August and weigh about 90g (3¼oz) at birth. Fed by their mother for the first month, they grow rapidly. Some may live as long as 10 years, but most of them die in infancy. As many as 85 per cent may not reach their first birthday, particularly where large numbers live in close proximity, reducing the amount of food available. However, the average number of youngsters that survive is about six per year for each

Hares on the move

Mountain hares often travel over mountain terrain to feed at night. They move with a slow, loping gait. If disturbed, they can put on a sustained burst of speed, sufficient to outpace most predators on the steep slopes.

LOSS OF HABITAT

Upland areas came under considerable pressure during the 1970s. In several key areas, heather moorland was lost at a rate of up to 4 per cent per year. One reason was a tax loophole that encouraged investment in large-scale forestry on marginal land. Many areas of potential mountain hare habitat were therefore lost to plantation forestry as a result of grant-aided conifer planting.

IMPACT OF LIVESTOCK

Another major threat to the hare's heather moorland habitat comes from sheep. Subsidies paid to farmers encourage them to keep large numbers of sheep. The impact of such livestock on moorland results in the spread of coarse grasses at the expense of heather, the main food of the hare. Sheep also nibble the vegetation so short that there is nowhere for the hare to build its forms to hide from predators or shelter from the wind and rain.

The mountain hare thrives best in heather moorland. Indeed, it is one of the few British mammals confined to a single habitat type. This is what makes mountain hares so vulnerable to changes

in moorland management or loss of heather habitat. Heather forms 50 per cent of the hare's diet, supplemented mainly by mountain grasses, such as *Agrostis* and *Deschampsia*. The hares prefer to eat short heather as it regrows after the moor has been burnt, but they need older, taller heather for shelter.

GAME SHOOTING

Currently the mountain hare has no legal protection. It may be shot for sport or for meat and some gamekeepers kill hares because they are a nuisance to deerstalkers – the hares dash off when disturbed, warning deer of the stalker's approach. Nevertheless, the mountain hare relies on gamekeeping for its survival. This is because mountain hares prosper on moors managed for red grouse, where small patches of heather are burned at intervals of several years. This sort of management increases the number of grouse for shooters,

▲ *Mountain hares have to keep a wary eye open for predators. Their large, widely spaced, bulging eyes give them virtually all-round vision.*

and it also benefits the mountain hare – moors that are good for grouse are good for mountain hares.

So, in many ways, the future of the mountain hare is linked to the red grouse's wellbeing. Many workers are needed to manage a piece of moorland for grouse. The cost of paying such a large workforce is only worthwhile so long as grouse shooting continues to be popular, and therefore profitable. Should that sport decline or be banned, the moorland habitat may degrade, or be put to alternative uses. For this reason, a ban on 'blood sports' could have a serious impact on the mountain hare. The grouse and hares would be spared from being shot, but the price they would pay is the loss of most of their best habitat.

Native ponies

Today's descendants of old wild herds search out lush pasture throughout the summer months. Unshod and ungroomed, these robust animals wander freely but survive only with the help of human intervention.

Thousands of years ago, truly wild horses and ponies colonised the land but, over the centuries, these creatures became extinct and various present-day breeds have taken their place. The Exmoor pony is probably the closest surviving relative of the ancient stock, although the wild ponies that inhabit the New Forest in Hampshire have been present since Saxon times.

Today, native pony herds are managed by humans. New blood from domestic stock has been introduced over the years to improve their commercial value, so most native ponies in the British Isles are now mixed in terms of their genes.

The strict definition of a pony is based on height at the shoulder – under 14.2 hands, or 1.47m (4ft 10in) – and on build. Compared to

▼ *Once the hunting ground of kings, the New Forest has been home to wild ponies since the reign of King Canute (or Cnut) from 1016 to 1035. Foals are born in May and June and are fiercely protected by their mothers.*

Shetland pony – island dweller

Shetland ponies originate from the wild, open islands to the north of the Scottish mainland. Nowhere is far from the sea, and the islands are lashed by wind and rain, even in summer. There is little shelter in this treeless landscape, so the ponies must be robust and hardy. The soils are poor and support grass that is not very nourishing – some of the ponies even visit the shore to eat seaweed.

Perhaps due to their relatively impoverished diet, Shetland ponies did not develop into large animals and, as a result, are a miniature breed. Another theory is that they are descended from dwarf ponies similar to Exmoors.

Ponies were brought to Shetland perhaps as much as a thousand years ago to assist in settling the islands. By about 1800, they were being exported back to the mainland as mounts for children. In 1847, child labour was abolished in British coal mines and suddenly there was a great demand for tiny Shetland ponies to replace them, pulling carts of coal in the cramped underground conditions. The effect was to reduce the pony population on the islands by half, from a maximum of about 10,000.

The ponies were bred on the mainland and by the 1950s there was little need for further exports, so the breed went into decline. However, good management of the ponies has ensured that they have not become extinct in their Shetland home. Today, several hundred of them survive there.

horses, ponies tend to be stockier, with shorter legs in proportion to their bodies, which means they take shorter strides. Pony foals are not so gangly looking as horse foals.

Although they roam freely across the open hills and moors, all of Britain's native ponies belong to someone. Those in the New Forest are owned by local people who hold commoner's rights to graze them on open land in the forest. New Forest and Exmoor ponies are rounded up every autumn to establish ownership and to check on the animals' welfare. Weak and sick ponies receive veterinary treatment and, if the herd is growing too large to be sustainable, any surplus animals are removed and sold.

GRAZING ANIMALS

Grass forms more than three-quarters of the summer diet of native ponies. With muscular jaws and large, square-crowned teeth that grow throughout their lives to compensate for being worn away by the tough food, they are adapted to eating large quantities of it. However, ponies are less effective than cows at digesting grass, which is why pony droppings are fibrous, containing a high proportion of matter that has not been completely digested. Unlike cows, ponies are not ruminants – that is, they do not have a multi-chambered stomach that allows them to digest food several times, with the aid of micro-organisms, regurgitating it for further chewing each time. Like all horses, ponies have a much simpler digestive system with a voluminous intestine that contains a large chamber, called a caecum, stocked with the micro-organisms that assist digestion.

Ancient breed

The ancestor of the domestic horse – and hence ponies – is thought to be Przewalski's horse of Asia. The true wild horses that lived in Britain in the company of woolly mammoths at the end of the last Ice Age were probably akin to this species. They died out about 9500 years ago as the climate improved, habitat was lost and the herds came under pressure from early humans. Later, they were replaced by domestic horses imported during the Iron Age.

It is possible, but unlikely, that Exmoor ponies are direct descendants of the original wild horses. It is more probable that they are a mixture of wild and domestic stock that has roamed freely for thousands of years – they are certainly the most ancient of the various types of wild pony found in Britain and Ireland. Only about 180 purebred Exmoors are left on the 17,000 hectares (42,000 acres) of Exmoor moorland and they are accompanied by increasing numbers of crossbred animals.

With incisor teeth in both upper and lower jaws, ponies are able to graze the turf short and tight, almost like a lawnmower. The turf is often nibbled so close that it contains very few plant species other than grass, because only grass can tolerate this treatment. This is especially true of areas where large herds gather.

FINDING FOOD

In dry summers, when the grass begins to dry out and its nutritional value declines, ponies have to diversify their feeding patterns and seek out other vegetation, often beside streams. They search for the best places to graze, selecting areas where the grass is lushest.

◀ *Stocky Dartmoor ponies are probably descended from Exmoors and are perfectly adapted to survival on steep, rock-strewn slopes. Wild ponies have lived on Dartmoor for at least a thousand years.*

In winter, however, ponies are often forced to find other sources of food. From autumn onwards, moorland and mountain ponies can be seen nibbling heather, moss, leaves and shrubs such as bramble and gorse, while in the New Forest, some animals even resort to eating spiky holly leaves. Ponies like to eat acorns and may spend hours nosing about among fallen leaves under the oaks in search of this energy-rich food.

Instinctively, they tend to avoid leaving their dung on the best grazing land. Often ponies use the same places year after year and the animals all copy each other and deposit their dung well away from good feeding areas. These communal latrines may also serve, to some extent, as territorial markers.

SOCIAL GROUPS

Native ponies live in small groups of females and immature animals led by a dominant mature male. Stallions are highly territorial and

▲ *Smell plays a vital role in the social world of ponies. It enables stallions to identify mares in heat and to keep track of potential rivals. Meeting for the first time, these Welsh Mountain ponies sniff each other.*

can be aggressive, especially in the breeding season. On the other hand, several stallions have been known to share the same grazing. The mares have a clear hierarchy based on seniority. The older ones are dominant and often take over as group leaders if there is no stallion present. Subordinates move aside to allow dominant animals to pass or feed, and the highest-ranked ponies often deposit their own dung or urine on top of that produced by other members of the group.

Ponies spend most of their time standing up, sometimes for several days at a stretch – they can even sleep on their feet. In late summer especially, groups of ponies may be seen standing close to each other

Running wild

Most Exmoor ponies are born in spring, which gives the foals plenty of time to grow and get fit for the winter. This is a time of sunshine and green grass, and the foals spend long periods playing. They caper wildly through the herd on their spindly legs, galloping as fast as they can.

for long periods, flicking their tails. This behaviour seems to be a way of gaining some protection from biting insects. By standing in groups, head to tail, ponies can swish flies away from each other. This is a useful consequence of living in groups, and probably encourages the animals to congregate and be sociable each day.

Confrontation is rare among ponies. Members of the herd frequently nuzzle each other and indulge in mutual grooming, although there may be the occasional dispute between individuals. Aggressive behaviour includes baring the teeth, sometimes even biting, and moving towards another animal with the neck outstretched and ears held flat. If these threats are ignored, the pony may spin around and kick out with both hind feet.

BREEDING BATTLES

The breeding season begins when the ponies moult their thick winter coats at about Easter time. Mares can breed when they are two years old, but many do not do so until later. They are receptive throughout the summer, but matings mostly occur early in the season. The stallions keep a close eye on their harems, constantly circling the

◄ *The Connemara may be black, bay, brown, dun or palomino, but grey is the most usual colour. The only indigenous breed in Ireland, these hardy ponies survive on a diet consisting mainly of rough grass.*

mares and preventing them from wandering off. Sometimes, other stallions may attempt to steal mares from the group and this is when very aggressive behaviour takes place. The competing stallions rear up on their hind legs, lash out with their front hooves and attempt to bite each other.

MARE AND FOAL

The mares are pregnant for 11 months and most foals are born from March the following year. Births usually take place at night or around dawn and are over very quickly, often within an hour. In another hour the leggy foal is able to stand up. The mares often mate again soon afterwards, and as they are capable of breeding well into the summer, some will conceive late, which results in foals being

▼ *For most of the year, Exmoor ponies live in small herds of up to 12 or so animals. Although they are free to roam over large tracts of moorland, most remain within an area of about 50 hectares (125 acres).*

born in September, or even later, the following year. These young ponies stay with their mothers throughout winter and continue to suckle until spring.

Mares do not normally produce a new baby every year, but may have two foals in three years. However, the numbers of many native pony herds are affected or controlled by their owners and the way in which these people manage their animals. For instance, young ponies may be separated from their mothers and sold earlier than separation would occur naturally. To avoid distressing the animals, owners are not allowed to sell foals younger than four months old unless they are accompanied by their mothers.

HARDY SURVIVORS

Left to themselves, some native ponies live for more than 20 years, but most die younger than this. Moorlands can be harsh places. In winter, bitingly cold winds and torrential rain are normal. Ponies that live in such environs must endure the weather, day and night.

All they can do to protect themselves is seek the meagre shelter provided by deep valleys or clumps of trees and bushes.

A pony's main protection lies in its very thick winter coat. From August onwards, masses of additional fine hairs grow among the hair of the pony's summer coat. This creates an extremely dense mass about 4cm (1½in) deep and gives the animal the appearance of having much thicker legs and a fatter body. The longer hairs that overlie the woolly insulating layer help to direct rainwater away so that it runs down the hairs and drips off without wetting the pony's skin. Long hairs also channel water away from the face and areas of the body vulnerable to chilling when wet. The winter coat is so effective in insulating a pony's body that snow can rest on its back without being melted by body heat.

Superbly adapted to their outdoor existence, native ponies survive the winter on minimum rations until they shed their thick coat the following spring to roam their plentiful summer grazing grounds.

The stoat

A fast-moving predator, the stoat lives on moorland where other hunting animals find conditions difficult. It has sharp teeth and a big appetite and, despite its small size, can kill prey several times larger than itself.

A glimpse of chestnut-coloured fur is all most people ever see of a stoat, as it runs across a country road, yet these animals occur throughout Britain and Ireland, and there are probably more of them than there are of any other mammalian predator. Prior to their annual breeding period, nearly half a million stoats are estimated to populate the country, although numbers fluctuate depending on the prevalence of their main prey, the rabbit. While stoats are sparsely distributed, they can be found in many different habitats where food and shelter are available, but compared to weasels they survive better on moorland.

LITHE BODIES

Sleek and sinuous, stoats are from 25 to 45cm (10 to 18in) long, including up to 14cm (5½in) of thin tail. The sexes look alike except that males are around 50 per cent heavier than females. The stoat's summer coat of rich brown is offset by a cream or yellowish white belly. The tail is tipped with a characteristic black brush, which bristles when the animal is disturbed or excited. In areas where snow is usual in the colder months, the stoat's fur turns white, providing effective camouflage.

Stoats leave few signs and it is difficult to find evidence of their presence. Pawprints can sometimes be seen in mud or in freshly fallen snow. Their five-toed tracks are about 1.5cm (⅝in) wide by 2cm (¾in) long for the forepaws, and 2.5cm (1in) wide by 4cm (1½in) long for the hind paws.

Stoats mark out their territories with thin, finely twisted droppings – known as scats – about 4 to 8cm (1½ to 3in) long, often containing the remains of fur and feathers. Their nests are hard to spot, usually located in crevices in rocks, trees and stone walls. They also usurp the nests and burrows of other animals, often moving in once they have killed and eaten the previous resident.

DEDICATED PREDATORS

As fast-moving creatures, stoats use a lot of energy. This is not just because of their speed but also because it takes energy to keep warm and their

◄ *A dry stone wall bordering a field makes an ideal base for a stoat. These animals are often seen in the north and west of Britain, where many such walls have been built, but this may be because the countryside is quite open there, making stoats easier to observe.*

long, thin shape means that they lose body heat rapidly. As a result, these small carnivores are voracious predators and eat up to one third of their own body weight every day.

Although their main prey are rabbits, which may make up over half their diet, small mammals, such as mice and voles, as well as eggs, nestlings and adult birds, are also taken. Stoats will occasionally eat rats and even squirrels. They are strong swimmers, so water birds do not escape the stoat's attentions.

When they are searching for food, stoats check every nook and cranny for signs of a potential meal. They rush about wildly, nosing under every grassy tussock and popping up and down rabbit burrows. When they find a mouse or other small item of prey, it is killed with a swift bite to

▲ *In late autumn, a young stoat leaves its home base to go in search of a new territory – a risky venture for inexperienced youngsters.*

White winters

Northern stoats respond to snowy winters by adopting an all-white coat, known as ermine, for camouflage. The stoat's winter fur is famous for its use in the ceremonial robes of royalty.

As temperatures drop in autumn and the days grow shorter, the stoat's brain sends out signals to the relevant cells to cut off supplies of pigments to the growing fur, and so the new coat grows white. If temperatures rise while the new coat is growing, pigment supplies can be turned on again. In changeable climates the stoat's fur can be part-pigmented, which gives it a mottled or pied appearance. White winter stoats are commonly seen in Scotland, north-western England and Wales. Occasional ermines and pied coats are found as far south as Wiltshire and Essex, but stoats in southern England usually remain brown in winter.

bite, or whether they die of the sheer fright of being attacked. Either way, the stoat's hunting prowess is enough to warrant its reputation as an efficient killer. One problem with killing rabbits is that it is dangerous to eat them out in the open where they are caught. Here, stoats are at risk from crows and birds of prey, so they often drag large food items considerable distances, to be eaten safely under cover of a hedge or among boulders.

Their predatory skill has brought them into conflict with humans, and stoats have been trapped and killed for many years. Gamekeepers still set traps in an attempt to control stoat numbers and reduce predation on the nests of gamebirds. Stoats are not a protected species so, while trapping is governed by various regulations, it is legal. What upsets game and poultry keepers is the stoat's habit of killing more than it can eat at the time. If they stumble on a hen house or pheasant pen, stoats often kill as many birds as possible. This practice has led to the belief that stoats kill for pleasure, but really they are attempting to provide for times when food is hard to come by. If they have the opportunity, they will drag dead prey away and hide it in a safe place.

the back of the neck. Stoats have extremely sharp teeth which easily penetrate the prey's skin.

Larger prey animals are more of a challenge, and when attacking rabbits and adult gamebirds, these small predators risk serious injury.

However, stoats are undeterred, often tackling adult rabbits up to six times their own weight, sometimes 'charming' their prey by swaying and inching forward sinuously. It is hard to tell whether rabbits and other large animals are killed by the stoat's

Hunting tactics

Rabbits are easily distracted by unusual activities in their field of view. A stoat exploits this natural curiosity to deceive a rabbit into allowing a fatally close approach.

Delayed implantation

Stoat reproduction includes a process known as delayed implantation. Stoats mate in the summer and the female's eggs are fertilised immediately. However, the fertile cells then enter a kind of suspended animation until the following spring, when they finally implant in the uterus and develop as normal. Gestation lasts only three to four weeks, but there can be a delay of as much as 11 months between mating and births.

The benefits are unclear, but to make up for this delay, female stoats have evolved to be extraordinarily precocious. Shortly after giving birth, adult females become sexually receptive and will choose a new mate. At around the same time, the young female kits become sexually mature (at just five weeks after their birth). Even though they are not yet weaned and have still to open their eyes and are helpless, they may mate with the same male as their mother. It is not uncommon for female kits to mate at just three to four weeks, before they are sexually mature.

Inbreeding is usually avoided because male stoats rarely live long enough (the nine or so months from mating to birth) to have any contact with their own offspring.

SIZE AND SURVIVAL

Evolution has given stoats an advantage over other, larger predators – stoats are small enough to pursue their prey right into their burrows. Rabbits can flee from foxes and buzzards, but there is no escape from a stoat. Even voles and mice, usually safe in their narrow tunnels, can be chased by the smaller female stoats. Their diminutive body size means, however, that they can, in turn, be taken by foxes, birds of prey and even domestic cats.

The black tip of a stoat's tail is, in fact, an adaptation to confuse birds of prey, such as kestrels, by deflecting attention away from the stoat's body. The stoat raises its tail at the last minute as the bird swoops down, in an effort to make it miss its target.

◄ *A young stoat takes hesitant steps away from the nest. Inexperienced individuals are often caught by cats and other predators, but still put up a fierce fight with their sharp teeth and claws.*

to solid food, the female stoat must spend more of her time foraging to bring back enough food for the young. Eventually, they learn to fend for themselves and become more independent, until they finally leave the nest and go their separate ways to find their own territories. Most family groups break up when the young are between four and six months old.

Young stoats have a difficult time when they leave the nest, and many do not survive beyond their first year. Average life expectancy is between 11 and 18 months, although occasionally an individual may live for up to ten years. Most animals die before they get a chance to breed successfully. Predation, trapping by gamekeepers, parasites and road traffic all take their toll on the young animals. However, the most important cause of death is often starvation. If the young stoats cannot secure and defend territories that contain enough prey, they will not last long in the adult world.

To obtain enough food, stoats need large territories. A male can occupy from 20 to more than 100 hectares (50–250 acres) – a big area for such a small animal. The territory's size depends on how plentiful and nutritious the food supply is. The male will defend his patch against other 'floating' males, usually young animals that do not have their own fixed territories.

The male's area contains several, smaller female ranges and he goes to great lengths to defend these potential mates. In spring and summer, dominant male stoats wander well beyond their usual range in order to track down as many mates as possible.

To compete with other males and to maintain territories, male stoats have an incentive to grow as large as possible. It is a tricky balancing act, however, because young male stoats that grow too big too quickly find that they cannot keep up with the energy required to sustain themselves and they are vulnerable to starvation early on in life.

Females also have limits to the size they can attain. If they grow too large, they will not be able to chase voles and other small prey into their burrows. Even when pregnant, female stoats have to maintain a sleek, lithe figure. For this reason, stoat babies, called kits, are born tiny and helpless. Litters are large, up to 12, and as soon as the kits are born, the mother's food requirements increase dramatically, not least because the male stoat plays no part in the rearing of the young.

Initially, all her energy goes into producing enough milk and keeping the kits warm. When she leaves the nest to forage for herself, the kits slow down their metabolism, lowering body temperature to conserve energy until she returns. As they grow and are weaned on

Packs of stoats

These animals are frequently reported to hunt together, and sometimes stories circulate of people or dogs being chased by packs of aggressive stoats. However, stoats are not social animals, and these groups almost invariably turn out to be litters of young on their first forays into the adult world.

Stoats are fearless in self-defence, and will fight if cornered or if their young are threatened, but there is no evidence to suggest that stoats have any predisposition to unprovoked attacks on humans. It is probably the playful nature and insatiable curiosity of juvenile stoats that give rise to these somewhat fanciful stories.

DECLINING POPULATION

When the viral disease myxomatosis reached epidemic proportions in Britain in the 1950s, most of the country's rabbits were wiped out. Stoats lost their main prey so their populations suffered, too. Rabbit numbers recovered from the disease and are now increasing, but stoats, despite being fast breeders able to take advantage of good conditions, do not generally seem to be benefiting from this increase in food.

Intensive farming may be one reason for this, because it leads to a reduction in rodents and small birds, although these form a smaller proportion of the stoat's diet than rabbits do. Eating poisoned rats and other rodents may be a threat. Some are deliberately put down by gamekeepers but stoats may also ingest insecticides and pesticides that have killed the rodents' prey. Another cause of decline may be increased competition with foxes.

Improvements in countryside management and the introduction of sensitive farming methods may prevent a more serious stoat decline, and give these lively predators a secure future.

▲ *If her nest is disturbed, a mother stoat will protect her young. She may pick up her babies and run away with them to a safe place. They are clamped firmly in strong jaws, held behind the large, sharp canine teeth.*

Stoat or weasel?

Stoats are frequently confused with weasels – both move fast and are small, long and thin with a brown back and a pale belly.

However, stoats are typically much larger than weasels. A stoat is about the size of a small squirrel, while a weasel is about twice the length of a mouse.

Weasels do not have a black-tipped tail and the stoat's tail is much longer. A good rule of thumb is that if the tail is very noticeable, it is probably a stoat, especially in a moorland or upland area, where stoats are more common than weasels.

A close look reveals that the line where the darker back fur meets the pale belly is straight in stoats but crooked in weasels. In Ireland stoats do have an irregular belly line like a weasel's, but then there are no weasels in Ireland. However, the stoat sub-species of the Isle of Man and Islay and Jura in the Inner Hebrides also have an irregular belly line like a weasel's.

The wild goat

Hardy and adaptable, goats are capable of surviving on a meagre diet. Their ability to scale rocky slopes and crags allows them to graze on vegetation that other animals cannot reach.

Goats were among the first animals to be domesticated, around 9500 years ago in the Middle East. They proved invaluable for their skins, milk and meat. Brought to Britain during the Neolithic period, their bones have been found dating back 4500 years. Over the centuries, escapees from domestic herds adapted to life in the wild and established their own feral groups. Today, their descendants still display characteristics of primitive ancient breeds, such as horns and upright ears, which have been lost in modern domestic goats.

Wild goats are agile creatures and most live on craggy cliffs and hillsides, often more than 300m (1000ft) above sea level. On such

▼ *Undeterred by steep ground or broken, unstable terrain, wild goats venture on to high mountain slopes during the summer months. Family groups graze on the fresh growth of upland plants.*

rough terrain, they are not a nuisance to farmers because crops are not grown there and goats are generally left alone. In severe winters, they may have to retreat to lower levels, but they soon return to their favoured steep slopes and rocky ledges when the weather improves. Some herds share the same ground as sheep and the two species co-exist peacefully.

HEARTY EATERS

Goats will eat any vegetation that they can reach, but are especially fond of fresh grasses, leaves and sedges. In winter, they will eat shrubs, even prickly gorse. Unlike sheep, goats eat bracken and even small conifer trees. They may rear up on their hind legs to nibble leaves, something that sheep do not attempt.

The goat's complex digestive system requires the animals to consume large amounts of food and then rest while the millions of microbes in their stomachs attack the plant material. Like sheep, goats are ruminants, periodically regurgitating a ball of semi-digested material and chewing it again, which is known as 'chewing the cud'. When the food is swallowed for a second time, it passes to further chambers before progressing to the true stomach and intestines. This complicated arrangement enables ruminants to consume food that would otherwise be indigestible.

During the summer goats alternate between short periods of feeding and chewing the cud, while during the winter months they eat in the morning and ruminate while resting in the middle of the day.

HERD BEHAVIOUR

In some places, the male goats, which are called billies, stay with the females, known as nannies, throughout the year, but elsewhere the billies live in small single-sex

herds, tending to associate with those of similar age. In such bachelor herds, the oldest and biggest animals are dominant.

Nanny goats usually wander off alone to give birth to their young, known as kids, and then join other females to form small herds. Family groups of nannies and their offspring from the current and previous years tend to stick together and are occasionally joined by a billy.

The groups are led by the oldest female and have separate home territories. These may be small where food is plentiful but the average size

▲ *Both male and female goats have horns that rise up from the forehead and curve backwards. Males have the largest horns, reaching an average of 39cm (15in) at three years old and 75cm (30in) at 10 years old.*

is three square kilometres (just over a square mile). Sometimes the goats range over more than twice this area. As the rut approaches in early autumn, larger groups may form, but the herds still comprise 8 to 15 animals only. At this time, billies disperse in search of females and social dominance is very important.

Just browsing

Goats will eat woody vegetation and strip bark off trees, a type of feeding called browsing, which can be very destructive. However, browsing can be put to good use where woody scrub is a nuisance. Goats will eat the unwanted shrubs and help to create an open environment suitable for wild flowers and butterflies.

On Ventnor Down on the Isle of Wight, goats have successfully cleared an invasion of dense, non-native shrubs from the steep slopes. The plants would have been very difficult to remove by any other method. However, thanks to these goats, many native plants and animals have now been restored to the area.

High-ranking billies stare balefully at rivals until the rivals back down. If intimidation does not work, the billy lowers his head in an explicit threat. If this is also ignored, the two males ram their heads together, trying to take the blow on their horns and at the same time push their opponent off balance. Two stubborn billies, neither of which will give way, may spend several hours driving their heads together.

Dominant billies regularly indulge in a pungent form of self-advertising by urinating on themselves. A male will often squirt his urine so that it sprays on to his beard. He will then rub up against trees and rocks in his territory, transferring the unmistakable odour. The strong smell ensures that inferior animals get wind of the male goat early enough so they can flee and avoid a fight.

YOUNG GOATS

Nannies usually give birth to one kid in March, five months after mating. Twins are uncommon and, if born, it is rare for both to survive. The newborn kid shelters in a small hideaway among rocks or in dense vegetation. Nowadays goats have little to fear from predators, since wolves are extinct and eagles are no longer widespread in Britain, but instinct ensures that the nannies look after their young by hiding them well. The female stays close to her

offspring for several days. Gradually, she moves farther away and soon the kid is able to follow her. Nannies continue to suckle their young for up to six months.

Kids are very vulnerable in the days following their birth. At least half of them die of starvation or disease before the end of summer. In severe or prolonged winters, the

mortality rate may be high, wiping out almost all the young and several older animals as well. Milder winters mean that many more goats will survive. Provided the young goats get through their first winter, they can look forward to a relatively long life. Many live to be six or more years old, and some reach the grand old age of 10 years.

◀ *The sure-footedness of the goat family is legendary. A goat will clamber up precipitous slopes and take death-defying leaps with absolute confidence. In order to satisfy their voracious appetites, wild goats rear up on their hind legs, stand on convenient rocky outcrops and even climb trees to reach sources of food.*

▶ *For a male goat, part of the ritual of the rut involves trying to intimidate rivals. If the glaring eyes and aggressive posturing fail to impress, billies resort to head-butting to establish supremacy.*

The pine marten

A nocturnal creature, the agile pine marten bounds through northern forests in a solitary hunt for food, equally at home on the ground or in the trees. This shy creature remains a rare sight despite an increase in its numbers.

The pine marten is one of the native mammals of Britain. Bones found at archaeological sites confirm that it has been present for at least 10,000 years. As recently as 200 years ago it was still widespread throughout mainland Britain, from northern Scotland to the south coast. It lived in the Isle of Wight and even on the fringes of London.

The animal's fine fur and the ease with which it could be snared made it attractive to trappers, and zealous gamekeeping in the 19th century was another devastating blow. As a result, pine marten numbers rapidly dwindled. The species had already become extinct in some English counties by about 1800, and by the 1920s pine martens remained relatively numerous only in north-west Scotland, where there were few people to trouble them.

However, from the 1930s pine marten numbers and distribution showed a steady increase, at least in Scotland. By the mid-1980s, they had returned to Tayside and the Strathclyde region. Natural barriers and heavily built-up areas have made further expansion difficult but not impossible and today there are probably around 3500 pine martens in Scotland.

Meanwhile, a few pine martens were still to be found farther south. Even now there are persistent

▶ *Always keeping a lookout for prey, the pine marten is also alert to possible danger, although its main enemy is man.*

Home range

The pine marten seems to prefer regions that combine large expanses of mature woodland with patches of open grass. This ensures plenty of logs, undergrowth and bushes for cover and shelter in harsh weather. Grassy glades are also favoured by the voles that are the marten's main prey.

Pine martens are particularly associated with conifer forests but, to some extent, this is forced upon them because conifer plantations are so extensive, especially in Scotland, offering large areas where the animals are relatively safe from gamekeepers. However, pine martens will also live on open moorland and hillsides and even in coastal areas.

Historically, English populations of martens were not restricted to conifer forests and were probably found in a wide variety of habitats.

reports of martens being seen, or found dead, in northern England, mainly in the Lake District, Northumberland and north Yorkshire. They never became completely extinct in Wales either, although evidence of their presence is scarce. Reports by reliable observers indicate that some do still live in parts of Wales and northern England, but the total number must be very low indeed, probably fewer than a hundred. It is by no means certain whether these scattered remnants will die out or increase their numbers sufficiently to form viable, secure breeding populations.

SLENDER HUNTER

The pine marten is an elusive, swift-moving creature and most sightings are no more than glimpses. At such times the animal resembles a thin cat, but with much shorter legs and a very dark brown coat. Unlike a cat, however, it has a thick furry tail. This is dark, and not banded as in a wildcat. When a marten moves quickly, it uses a bounding action, its back arched high, very different from a cat or any other animal that might be confused with it, except perhaps an otter, mink or polecat. Another distinctive feature is its ears, which are triangular and prominent, about 4cm (1½in) long and with pale edges that emphasise their shape.

WANDERING MALES

Males have larger home territories than females, bordered by natural boundaries such as streams and hedgerows. These boundary areas are often densely marked with droppings.

Martens may travel more than 10km (6 miles) in a night, searching for food. Where food is abundant, the animals can restrict themselves to smaller ranges and this increases the potential population density of the region.

During the breeding season, martens trespass on to each other's territories looking for mates but, despite any consequent aggression, fights are rare. Their razor-sharp teeth can deliver a painful and possibly dangerous nip and they are careful to avoid being bitten during confrontations. They are more likely to express their hostility though growls and hissing noises, often spitting like angry cats. Most of the time they simply avoid each other, aided by the scent marks that, left in prominent places, help them to keep track of their neighbours.

Martens make their dens in a variety of places – tree holes, hollow logs, cavities among boulders – and often have several dens within their home territory. They may use nestboxes intended for owls or ducks, and sometimes choose outbuildings. Normally they are nocturnal, but in the higher latitudes of Scotland summer nights are brief and it may not get dark until nearly midnight, with sunrise barely four hours later. This makes it difficult for them to carry out all their activities in darkness, especially females trying to collect food for themselves and their young, so martens may occasionally be seen out in daylight, especially in May and June.

MIXED DIET

The pine marten's distinctive droppings betray exactly what it has been eating. The droppings are up to 12cm (4¾in) long, black and twisted like a rope. Often slimy, they dry out in the sun and stay in one piece if they contain fur or feathers. When the animal has been eating mainly berries, its droppings quickly disintegrate in the rain into heaps of pips and fragments of fruit skin.

This shows that the pine marten is not just a carnivorous hunter but also feeds on plant matter, eating rowan berries, raspberries, and even fungi.

Wary hunters

Despite their agility in the trees, pine martens hunt mainly on the ground. However, this makes them vulnerable and they will quickly retreat up a tree if danger threatens.

Arboreal activity

The pine marten is a member of the weasel family. Uniquely among its relatives, it has semi-retractable claws. These show up prominently in photographs and leave distinct claw marks when the animal crosses soft mud, damp sand or snow, but they retract far enough to stay very sharp. This not only allows the pine marten to run very fast along the ground, but also to scramble up smooth tree trunks and branches.

However, unlike a squirrel, it cannot rotate its ankles to come down a tree head first, hanging by its back feet. Instead, it has to embrace the tree and let itself down tail first in a series of 'jumps', with the hind claws digging in to keep a grip. Despite this, it is a very agile creature that can climb, bound and jump among the branches with athletic ease.

As it works its way through the tree tops, the pine marten often discovers birds' nests and devours the eggs. It may also locate the dreys (nests) of squirrels and occasionally it will eat their young. The marten's agility and speed enables it to chase squirrels through the trees, and it may even catch the odd one now and again, especially inexperienced juveniles.

This has given rise to the myth that squirrels are the main food of pine martens, but in reality, chasing full-grown squirrels through the trees would be dangerous and use far more energy than could be obtained from the few actually caught.

In fact, the marten's main mammal prey consists of voles, particularly the field vole, which it catches in woodland glades and on the grassy edges of forest tracks. A marten may eat its catch on the spot, or take it back to its den.

It is certainly not a ravenous killer, and pine martens probably do relatively little damage to gamebird populations. Their destruction by gamekeepers was more to do with prejudice against all predators other than humans, rather than any real threat they posed to grouse or pheasants.

However, martens will take advantage of poorly constructed chicken coops if they can squeeze their lithe, slim bodies through gaps in woodwork or around ill-fitting doors.

They also take a variety of small mammals from voles to young rabbits, as well as squirrels and young birds, which they catch in the trees. In winter they will eat carrion, scavenging the remains of small animals killed by the cold.

◄ *Each pine marten has a creamy bib under its chin, which varies in size, tint and shape. This enables individuals to be identified in the wild.*

BIRTH CONTROL

Pine martens mate in July or August, and the females give birth in March or April of the following year. This might suggest a pregnancy period of more than seven months, which would be a long time for a relatively small mammal. In fact, the pine marten operates what is called 'delayed implantation', whereby the fertilised egg begins development soon after mating but then stops growing for six or seven months. The egg then implants into the wall

Sense of smell

The pine marten gets its bearings by laying a scent trail. To find this again it must use its nose to identify where it is, even in broad daylight. The sweet musky scent left by the marten makes it fairly easy to track.

Although the pine marten is a superb tree climber, it also spends a good deal of time on the ground, like this one taking a drink at a lakeside. It can move fast over the terrain if it has to, using a bounding gait. The pine marten has been known to catch fish – it can swim, but rarely does so unless absolutely necessary.

of the womb to complete its development, taking about 30 days. An unusual system, it is nevertheless found in a variety of other mammals, including badgers and grey seals.

This adaptation ensures that the young are born at the most advantageous time of the year, and in the case of the pine marten, this is early summer. If it had a normal pregnancy period, it would need to mate during the winter when harsh weather and perhaps deep snow can make survival difficult enough without the added stresses of finding a mate. It is far more convenient and efficient for pine martens to find mates in summer, when they are active over wide areas. Delayed implantation also ensures that the babies are not born when the weather is still bad. They would be likely to starve if born in the winter.

The young are born blind and helpless, with sparse whitish fur and weighing about 30g (1oz). Their eyes open at about six weeks, but it is another month before they venture far from the den. Young pine martens become independent between three and four months old,

when they resemble their parents except for having rather spindly tails and thinner coats. Their fur thickens in time for winter.

SLOW BUILD-UP

Pine martens usually mate for the first time at two or three years old and produce one litter per year, of up to five young. They live at very low densities, with perhaps one animal to every 10 square kilometres (4 square miles), which means that the loss of just one or two to traps, illegal shooting, road accidents or natural mortality can leave a big gap in the population. This is one reason why pine martens disappeared from most of Britain relatively quickly and why their reappearance has been slow, despite complete legal protection in recent years.

An attempt to reintroduce the pine marten to certain parts of the country, effectively leapfrogging all the obstacles to its natural distribution, was made in 1980 when a dozen animals were released in Forestry Commission plantations near Dumfries in south-west Scotland. They survived and

Underground predator

The pine marten is an active hunter, and may even venture down burrows in search of young rabbits. Having killed its prey, the marten hauls it out by the ears, dragging the heavy weight between its front paws.

their numbers have increased. This population has spread, although not very far. There have also been some successful reintroductions in Ireland.

FUTURE PLANS

The pine marten is a prime candidate for reintroduction to parts of England as well, and studies are being made to find out whether this would be feasible and likely to succeed. It would be pointless and even cruel to release pine martens if they were likely to die out again as a result of persecution, trapping or road accidents.

Even in the remote regions of the far north, where the pine marten is relatively numerous, its survival rate and lifespan is by no means certain in the wild. If the species is to be reintroduced farther south, it is important to select areas where traffic density is low, and where the animals will be tolerated by local farmers and gamekeepers. If reintroduced animals have to face the dangers of traps, illegal poisons and busy roads, they may not be able to cope.

The habitat must also be suitable – Forestry plantations may not be ideal but other, apparently more natural, regions may be even less adequate. The challenge is made greater by the fact that, owing to its rarity and its elusive nature, the pine marten has not been studied very thoroughly. It remains a slightly mysterious animal.

▲ *For a marten, much of the day is spent sleeping before venturing out to search for food at dusk. The animal may look docile when waking up naturally, but it can be very fierce if disturbed, spitting and snarling like an angry cat.*

CHAPTER 4 • WATERSIDE AND COAST

The otter

A supple body, thick fur and webbed paws ensure that the otter is suited to life both in water and on land. Once on the verge of disappearing from England altogether, it is gradually returning to rivers and shores.

In the wild, otters are charming, playful animals, a joy to watch as they frolic among seaweed and rocks and on river banks – but very few people have ever seen a wild otter. They are nowhere near as common in England and Wales as once they were, although they are still fairly widespread along remote stretches of Scottish coastline, in sea lochs and estuaries. Unfortunately, otters disappeared from much of central and eastern England in the mid-1950s, largely due to the destruction of their habitat and pollution caused by pesticides. They are staging a comeback in Wales and south-west England but their recovery is slow.

FOLLOWING THE CLUES

Black, tar-like droppings on rocks and tree trunks beside rivers and on quiet beaches are a sure sign that an otter has been in the area recently. Tracks in the mud or soft sand are another clue. Otters' footprints are 6–7cm (2½–2¾in) long and show five toes, although the fifth toe is not always clear. Dog and fox prints have only four toes. Fresh tracks often show the marks of the webbing between the toes and claws.

▼ *A glimpse of an otter on a river bank, or resting at the water's edge, is a rare treat, especially during daylight hours. The animal will soon slip into the water and out of sight.*

Another telltale sign of an otter's presence is a well-used muddy chute worn through the vegetation down a steep bank into the water. No other animal is likely to create such a slide. Where slow-moving rivers meander through grassy fields, an otter may take a regular short cut across a bend, leaving a trail from one bank to the next. A partially eaten fish in the vicinity could possibly be the remains of an otter's meal.

An otter can travel over 10km (6 miles) in a night and males visit up to 80km (50 miles) of river in a year. Typically, one otter occupies a 10–15km (6–9 mile) stretch of river bank or lake side. Coastal otters usually have smaller territories, perhaps as little as 2km (1¼ miles) of shoreline. This may be because food is more abundant by the sea and rock-pool fish are easier to catch than bigger river fish. Mountain streams and lakes often have very few fish, and otters are thinly dispersed in these areas.

SWIMMING AND DIVING

Otters are adapted for an amphibious way of life – they rest and breed on land but catch most of their food in water. An otter is very sleek and agile, both underwater and at the surface. Its lithe body can twist and turn, changing direction swiftly. When swimming at the surface, the otter often creates a distinctive V-shaped wake, which extends from its muzzle.

The otter's fur is very dense, trapping air close to the skin, which helps to keep it warm, even in freezing cold water. As an otter dives smoothly out of sight, the pressure of the water squeezes some of this air out of the fur, leaving a giveaway trail of bubbles rising to the surface.

▲ An otter's fur is thick enough to keep it warm and dry when it swims in cold water. Even so, an otter usually spends no more than 20–30 minutes in the water before coming ashore to dry off.

Loss of some of the insulating layer of air causes a drop in body temperature and is one reason why otters normally dive in shallow water where the water pressure is low, so less air is forced out. On the other hand, the air in the fur also acts like an unwanted life jacket, making the

Vital senses

Otters rely mainly on touch and smell for catching prey. The prominent whiskers are vital sensory organs, especially at night or in murky water. The forward-facing eyes suggest that they have good binocular vision in daylight.

◄ *When a wet otter comes ashore, it shakes vigorously and rolls about in the grass to dry its fur quickly. If it hears anything alarming, it may sit up on its haunches, supported by its tail, to take a good look around.*

SAFE RETREAT

The otter is mainly active at night (except in parts of north-west Scotland and Shetland). It needs secluded lying-up places where it can rest in the day. An otter may have up to 30 different lairs around its territory – all within about 50m (165ft) of the water's edge – so that, after a night's hunting, it never has far to go to find a safe resting place. It often builds daytime underground dens, called holts, among riverside tree roots. Sometimes it makes a couch from grass and twigs as an above-ground den, known as a hover. In fine weather an otter may sleep out in the open among the rocks on the shore or on a river bank.

HUNTING AND FEEDING

Otters have an acute sense of smell, which they use to locate their prey, as well as to find each other and to detect danger. They are skilled predators and feed on a wide variety of prey, including fish, frogs and crustaceans, which they catch in the water. Occasionally, they also catch

Otter or mink?

The otter is often mistaken for the American mink, introduced into this country for the fur trade and now well established in the wild.

- Compared with a cat, the otter is noticeably larger and the mink smaller.

- The otter is a milk-chocolate colour, darker when wet; a mink's coat is usually dark brown all over, apart from a little white on the chin.

- The otter has a flat, broad head with prominent whiskers; the mink has a pointed muzzle.

- An otter's tail is long, cylindrical and tapered; the mink's is bushy, when dry.

- The otter is shy and rarely seen in daylight; the mink is bold and often seen during the day.

otter more buoyant, so it has to work harder to stay submerged. This energetic paddling means that an otter soon gets out of breath and needs to surface to take a gulp of air.

After swimming in sea water otters like to bathe in freshwater pools to rinse the salt from their fur and keep each hair clean and separate

mammals, such as rats and water voles, and some birds. Their hunting behaviour is very adaptable and they take advantage of whatever feeding opportunities arise. They grope in muddy water to find fish among tree roots, nuzzle submerged stones to catch crayfish hiding underneath and even seize moorhens sitting on their nests.

Checking the air

Before retiring to its den to rest, an otter warily checks that it's safe to do so by taking a good sniff of the area, tentatively raising its head and twitching its long whiskers.

▶ *A definite chute in the snow like this is a very good sign that an otter, or maybe even a family of otters, has been in the area lately.*

Most of the otter's diet consists of fish. An adult otter needs to eat about 20 per cent of its body weight in food every day. Normally, in shallow water, an otter chases its prey this way and that until the fish tires, then snatches it in its teeth. Shallow pools are best because the fish cannot get away easily and the otter can surface quickly and regularly to breathe. In deeper water, an otter approaches its prey from below, so the fish cannot see it coming.

Many dives end unsuccessfully. In water more than 2m (6½ft) deep, the otter may take as many as 12 attempts to catch anything. In shallow rock pools, it may be successful in a third of its dives, but then the prey, such as a blenny, is generally small and weighs only around 100g (3½oz). In lakes, the fish tend to be larger – an otter often takes eels weighing up to 500g (1lb 2oz). It only needs to catch about three fish of that size to satisfy its hunger for a whole day.

FIGHTING AND MATING

Otters usually live alone, unless the female is rearing a family of cubs. Adults rarely meet in the wild. When two rival males encounter one another, a fight may ensue. Fighting involves plenty of squealing and chasing, even some biting, until one of them concedes and runs away. The male and female only meet up to mate, attracted to each other when the female is fertile by a combination of scent and whistling. As a prelude to mating, there is often a period of courtship, when a male and female indulge in some energetic, flirtatious chases, romping about on land or in the water. They then mate, either on land or while

Growing up

Otter cubs develop a waterproof coat by the time they are two or three months old. Soon after, they start having swimming and hunting lessons from their mother. At first, some cubs are reluctant to take the plunge and may need a push. After swimming, the cubs re-scent each other by rubbing against the base of their mother's tail and spreading her scent over each other's fur. Tired out, they then curl up and fall asleep.

Otter spotting

Watching otters requires great patience. Finding signs that there is an otter about is much easier than catching sight of one. The clues are surprisingly obvious once you know what to look for. Otter droppings, called spraints, are the most common sign. These are smeared as territorial scent markers on rocks and logs above the water level in rivers, at the edge of lakes and under bridges. The spraints are small, 6–8cm (2½–3¼in) long and 1cm (½in) in diameter. You may see little clusters, with some spraints fresher than others. Recent ones look sticky and very black, like a patch of thick crude oil. Older, drier ones are grey and powdery, like ash on a burnt-away cigarette. Closer inspection reveals fragments of prey – fish bones, scales and bits of crayfish or crab shells. The only other droppings likely to be seen along the water's edge that resemble otter spraints are those of the mink. These are black, about 6cm (2½in) long, with a twisted tip, and also contain bones and shells. However, otter spraints have a curious oily smell, which is surprisingly sweet; mink droppings smell acrid in comparison. If you find evidence of an otter, sit quietly out of sight and wait since the creature may pass that way again.

swimming. Coupling can take up to half an hour. Afterwards, the two animals separate and return to their solitary lives. The male plays no part in raising the cubs.

FAMILY LIFE

Otters can breed at any time of the year, probably because British winters are relatively mild and food is never scarce. Most cubs are born between May and August. Females can bear a litter every year, but nearly half of them probably raise a family every other year. Gestation lasts about 62 days. During this time, the female otter digs an underground breeding den, known as a holt. She may select somewhere well away from water or along a small tributary rather than beside a big river. The site is always above the level likely to be reached by flood waters. She lines the holt with dry grass and moss to make a cosy chamber in which she gives birth to her cubs.

Usually there are two or three cubs, in a litter, although occasionally as many as five are born. At birth, otter cubs are pink with a thin fuzz of pale fur. They

measure about 12cm (4½in) in length and weigh just 100g (3½oz). For the first four or five weeks of their lives, the cubs are blind and utterly helpless. They are totally dependent on their mother for warmth and milk, suckling frequently and making little chirruping noises.

The cubs grow slowly, and at four or five weeks weigh about 700g (1lb 9oz). They start eating solid food when they are roughly seven weeks old, by which time their weight has increased to about 1kg (2lb 4oz).

In another three weeks they venture outside the holt to play. The cubs eventually leave home when they are 10–12 months old. The average number of young otters reared to independence is fewer than two per female per year, but the success rate may be higher in years when food is abundant.

JUVENILE CHALLENGES

The first few weeks out on its own are a testing time for a young otter. It has to get used to catching all its own food and find shelter during

Otter hunting

Until quite recently, otter hunting was a traditional rural pursuit. It was most popular in the 1930s, when about 400 otters were killed every year. Even as recently as the 1950s, there were a dozen active otter hunts. Each operated for 40–50 days every year, killing an average of 200 otters between them.

The hunters formed a line across a small river and, armed with long poles, walked slowly upstream, thrashing the water and forming a barrier to prevent the otter from doubling back. Otter hounds would forge ahead, seeking the scent and signs of otters in burrows and under tree roots along the banks. When a find was made, the chase could last for an hour or more. Sometimes the otter got away, but often it did not. This beautiful animal was hunted mainly for sport although its reputation for being a nuisance to anglers, and salmon fishermen in particular, was often used to justify the culls.

the day as well as seek out and establish a new territory for itself. Inevitably this means travelling some way from its mother's home area. Many young otters die at this stage, either through malnutrition or from being run over as they cross roads looking for a suitable place to live.

Fewer than half the cubs live to see their fourth birthday, but those that do survive their first two or three years have a reasonable chance of living for six or seven years. Perhaps one otter in a hundred reaches ten years of age.

FUTURE PROSPECTS

The main threats to all otters are a shortage of food and the ever-present risk of being run over. Oil spills are another hazard for those living in coastal waters, especially around Shetland. Some get caught up and drown in eel traps. In the past, many were killed or rendered infertile by pesticides. Pesticides are less of a problem nowadays, but eating fish contaminated by chemical spills and effluents may become a real threat as otters begin to recolonise rivers in industrial areas. The positive news is that many river authorities are now

spending significant amounts of money on improving the water quality and fish stocks of their rivers. Some are also providing lying-up places where otters can rest during the day. Such measures will surely help otter numbers recover from an all-time low in the 1960s and 1970s. Already there are more otters living in Britain than in almost any other country in Europe.

▼ *Otters often prefer to hunt in streams and tributaries rather than in large rivers, because fish and other prey are easier to catch in shallow water.*

The water vole

The bustling activity of the water vole is all too rarely seen today, but conservation efforts aimed at protecting this shy mammal are starting to produce a small recovery in numbers in wetland reserves and on river banks.

In recent years it has become an increasingly rare privilege to see a water vole swimming near the river bank or to hear the distinctive plop of one taking to the water. Numbers have decreased drastically in the last 15 years or so, down from an estimated 7.3 million in 1990 to just 875,000 in 1998, but the water vole population has been in decline for much longer than that. It may not be too late to reverse the situation, however. Water vole conservation is important and worthwhile, not just because these are attractive and harmless creatures, but because their continued presence is a valuable indicator of a healthy and viable waterside habitat.

Rarely found far from fresh water in Britain, the water vole is markedly less aquatic in continental Europe. Indeed, in parts of southern Central Europe, water voles behave more like moles, often living in pastures and other farmland, and excavating and living in burrows. This behaviour has led to the species being regarded as a pest in some areas.

TUNNEL DWELLERS

Water voles normally live in an extensive system of burrows in river banks, inside which they construct nest chambers and line them with grass. A burrow system usually has at least one entrance below water level, which can be used without exposing the animal to view.

In the breeding season the animals may spend 60 per cent of their time in the burrow, and even more at other times of the year. Activity comes in bursts – at night as well as in the daytime – with a few hours rest in between.

Where burrowing is not possible, such as in reedbeds or areas of waterlogged soil, water voles may live among tussocky vegetation or weave rushes into a domed nest, about 30cm (12in) across.

◄ *When supplies of summer grasses and other fresh vegetation dwindle, water voles often feed on bark and roots. At other times of year, these are not among their favourite food.*

▶ *Water voles inhabit waterside areas, preferring river banks and pond margins that support a rich and varied plant life.*

Underwater swimmers

Most rodents are capable of swimming if they have to, but water voles are very much at home in the water. They take to it when alarmed, but they are by no means entirely safe there. Like most small aquatic animals and birds, water voles are vulnerable to attack from above and below. Their main predators are mink, stoats, herons and pike.

▼ *In good years, the breeding season can extend from March into October, which gives a healthy female time to raise as many as four litters. As soon as the young are weaned, the female is ready to breed again.*

BUSY BREEDERS

The young are born between March and September, or even October, after a pregnancy lasting around three weeks. Three or four litters may be produced in a season, with an average of five young in each. The blind, hairless babies weigh about 5g (⅛oz) at birth and grow rapidly, quadrupling their size within a fortnight, when they begin to emerge from the nest and learn to fend for themselves. They are fed by their mother for up to three weeks, but she may evict them when her next brood is born, by which time they are about half their adult size.

Some of the earliest young may be capable of breeding before the summer is out, so water voles have the capacity to produce large numbers of offspring in a year. However, their chances of surviving beyond six months are slim. As well as predators such as mink, water voles are in danger from owls and cats when moving to new territories. They suffer a high mortality rate at this time.

of bubbles. The vole has to visit the surface to breathe, which it often does under cover of vegetation where it cannot easily be seen.

LIVING SPACE

In winter, females with some of their offspring, and occasionally a few unrelated males, may nest together. In early spring, high population densities can occur in some places and 20 or more voles may congregate in less than half a kilometre (quarter of a mile) of river bank. As spring progresses, they begin to spread out and by May all the breeding females have an exclusive territory, which they defend. Each territory occupies about 75–130m (250–430ft) of water's edge. The males have larger ranges that may overlap the territories of several females.

During the breeding season, scent glands on the flanks become very enlarged and the animals scratch these with their hind feet. The males stomp their feet on the ground to mark it – a practice known as 'drum-marking' – and both sexes leave scent along their trails. This probably aids social recognition as well as marking territorial boundaries. On meeting, water voles may lash their tails and chatter their teeth. If a fight develops, they will grapple and bite each other, rolling over and over, sometimes causing serious wounds.

SIGNS OF LIFE

The activities of water voles are fairly conspicuous. Where they emerge from the water there may be a smooth wet patch, often forming a platform and sometimes with distinctive star-shaped prints – four toed from the forefeet and five toed from the hind feet. Droppings are oval, around 1cm (½in) long and greenish brown or black, depending on what the voles have been eating and how long ago they were deposited. The droppings tend to be left in small heaps – or latrines – near where the animals leave the water, and help to delineate territory.

Water voles can be seen by day sitting up like squirrels and nibbling food held in their paws. They eat mainly grasses, sedges, reeds, rushes and other waterside plants, and consume nearly 80 per cent of their own body weight each day. Uneaten remains are left in small heaps. Piles of sedge leaves or reed stems with the juicy parts missing are typical water vole leftovers. They gnaw the base of tall plants to bring them down, as a forester might fell a tree. The best parts are eaten and the rest abandoned.

Sometimes voles move away from the water's edge to graze grass or eat crops, leaving bald patches as evidence. Where water voles live in high densities, they may consume up

---

Those born early in the season are likely to live longer than young born later on, and in rare cases may survive to see a third summer.

GOOD SWIMMERS

Although water voles don't have webbed feet, they swim well. They often dive, but not very deep. Their soft fur traps a layer of air close to the skin and underwater the pressure forces some air out, creating a trail

---

Water vole or water rat?

Despite its country name of water rat, this enchanting animal is not a rat. The common brown rat, *Rattus norvegicus,* may be seen in similar waterside habitats, but there are several notable differences to help identify them.

Water voles have dark chestnut brown silky fur, with long glossy guard hairs projecting from the main coat,

whereas the common rat has coarse, grey-brown, rather shaggy fur and looks dull rather than glossy. The vole's face is chubby and rounded, with small hairy ears; the rat has a pointed nose and more prominent fleshy ears.

The vole's tail is thin and looks dark (because it is hairy) and extends for about half the length of the body. A

rat's tail is long – about three-quarters its body length – scaly and naked, so it looks pinkish grey.

Voles are seen in water or at the water's edge, and are mostly country animals. Rats are widely found in and around human habitations. When frightened, the vole dives from the bank with a 'plop', whereas rats slip silently into the water or dive in with a splash.

Underground network

Water vole burrow systems can be surprisingly complex, often having a number of chambers linked by a system of tunnels. When young are in the burrow, the parent vole may loosely seal the entrance with a wad of grass and perhaps also mud.

Entrances at water level are always in danger of flooding, and when the water table is particularly high the voles may not bother with a burrow at all. In such circumstances, they may build a nest above ground, in dense tussocks of grass or sedge. Seasonal flooding or bad weather has been known to drive water voles from their preferred waterside habitat. Away from water, they build more extensive burrow systems and live almost completely below ground.

to a fifth of all the plant growth in the area. In summer, they are known to harvest grasses and store them in their burrows for later consumption. In autumn and winter, when many plants are dead or dormant, voles often turn to eating fallen fruit, roots, bulbs and the bark of waterside trees, such as willow and alder.

SPECIES AT RISK

Water voles are prolific breeders and should not be threatened with dying out in Britain, yet there are disturbing signs that this is exactly what is happening.

The first National Water Vole survey, conducted in 1989–90, revealed that although the animal was still widespread, there seemed to be fewer numbers at each site than before and they appeared to have vanished altogether from about 70 per cent of places where they were known to have been present in the past. Even the otter's decline was not as dramatic. Worse still, a follow-up survey showed that the rate of decline had increased to about 90 per cent by 2000. Yet until recently this catastrophic state of affairs had scarcely been noticed.

Unless the causes of decline are understood, it is difficult to carry

out effective practical measures to stop water voles from dying out in Britain. Pollution is a possible culprit, although voles are almost entirely vegetarian and are therefore unlikely to be affected by insecticides and poisons that accumulate in prey. Disease is another possibility, but there is no evidence that water voles have been affected by any specific diseases. Neither have winters been so severe as to cause problems for semi-aquatic creatures. River engineering works have certainly destroyed much of its valuable habitat, but the vole should have been safe in small streams and ponds.

The most frequently cited culprit is the American mink. Originally introduced to British fur farms, from the 1950s onwards the animals began escaping, resulting in a steady build-up of numbers in the wild. Mink eat water voles, which share the same habitat and are often too slow both on land and in water to escape this lithe and amphibious predator. Once mink reach an area, water voles tend to vanish within a year or two. This observation led to the assumption that, since mink cannot easily be eradicated, the water vole was doomed to die out.

▲ *Water vole prints in the soft mud at the side of a pond or river show the four distinct toes of the forefeet.*

However, this forecast overlooks the fact that the water vole's decline has been going on for decades and began long before mink became widely established. The problem is more complex than predatory mink alone.

SHRINKING HABITAT

Research suggests that several interacting factors have probably contributed to the water vole's decline. The population is not spread evenly across the countryside. Instead, voles live on strips of land by the water's edge and if those strips are cut into short sections – by lining a river bank with concrete, for instance, or building along it – the vole population becomes fragmented. Each of these small colonies is vulnerable to chance events such as poor breeding (possibly brought on by stress, which causes females to produce male offspring only), floods drowning animals in their burrows, or physical damage to river banks by dredging machinery. Gaps between surviving groups widen and local vole populations become even more isolated and vulnerable. Mink arriving in such a pocket are quite likely to wipe out any remaining water voles.

In the past, water voles could have retreated into wet marshland but most such areas, especially beside lowland rivers (the best water vole habitat), have been drained to grow crops or provide better pasture. As a result, the water vole is restricted to a narrow band at the water's edge. Only here does the full range of plants on which it feeds continue to grow, but in this narrow strip there is nowhere to escape from prowling mink.

Water voles need a variety of vegetation to survive, especially in winter when many plants die back or the water freezes, preventing access to underwater plants. Waterside plants are naturally very diverse, but

if they are dredged out to improve water flow, or pollutants reduce the numbers of plant species, water voles find it increasingly hard to survive. Pollutants devastate plant life in two ways – either by killing the plants directly or doing so indirectly through a process called eutrophication (overfeeding), when a build-up of nitrates encourages a heavy surface growth of algae – known as a 'bloom' – that stops water plants growing.

These problems are less severe in reedbeds and marshland. Not only are there plenty of plants to eat all year round, but the dense reed stalks

▲ *An active water vole tends to be busy by day. Water voles like clean water and diverse vegetation, so evidence of a vole population suggests a healthy habitat.*

give water voles an escape route from mink. Perhaps the real problem for the water vole has been that this sort of refuge no longer exists in many lowland areas, leaving voles more vulnerable to predators. Now that the problems are better understood, however, it may be possible to try out various forms of habitat management so as to reduce the water vole's vulnerability.

Creatures of habit

Water voles consistently use the same route to enter and leave the water. Smooth platforms develop on the banks of the river where the vegetation is trampled or worn away.

CHAPTER 4 • WATERSIDE AND COAST

The mink

A waterside animal, the mink hunts most actively at night. With its long, athletic body, this carnivore is an excellent climber and swimmer and catches its prey on land and in water.

The mink is the first undomesticated carnivore from another country known to have adapted successfully to living wild in the British Isles. Resident for only the last few decades, the mink was first imported in 1929 from America by British fur farmers. Mink bred well in captivity and could be fed cheaply on unwanted animal waste produced, for example, by poultry farms.

The mink's fur is shiny and soft, and it also has a dense and fluffy underfur that protects it from cold when swimming. This underfur can be made into expensive coats and trimmings. Careful selection of animals for breeding allowed mink to be produced with different-coloured furs, ranging from silver-white to cream, as well as the natural dark chocolate-brown. The pale – called 'pastel' – mink furs fetched an especially high price.

ESCAPING INTO THE WILD

The mink industry expanded rapidly during the 1950s with the importing of large numbers of animals – often as many as 700 in a single shipment – from North America. By 1962 there were more than 700 mink farms in Britain, producing 160,000 pelts per year, a figure that quickly rose to more than a quarter of a million.

With so many animals being kept, often in poorly secured cages, it was inevitable that escapes would occur. Mink are athletic animals, able to climb well, and they also proved adept at squeezing through surprisingly small gaps. Those that

▼ *Basking in the sun, a mink surveys its territory. This is usually a stretch of river bank or an area around the edge of a lake or marsh. Mink may also live along the seashore, where their prey includes crabs, molluscs and small fish.*

escaped adapted well to living in the wild and, with farms scattered all over the country, right from the outset, mink began to colonise many areas of Britain and Ireland. The first confirmed reports of mink breeding in the wild came from Devon in the late 1950s. In the 1960s, the Ministry of Agriculture began a trapping campaign to eliminate them but despite the killing of a thousand or more each year – in addition to those trapped or shot by gamekeepers – the population continued to expand.

By 1971, mink were found in 41 counties in England and Wales, with many also living in different parts of Scotland and Ireland. Their spread into eastern England was slow but they are now common there, too. In less than half a century, the mink became one of Britain's most prevalent carnivores. A 1995 estimate showed a population of about 110,000, making the mink far more numerous than either the otter or the polecat. Since then, however, there has been a massive decline in the mink population. In 2004 it was estimated at about 37,000 – a result, perhaps, of the increase in otters which occupy the same waterside territory.

NEW PREDATOR

Much controversy surrounded the mink's successful adaptation to living wild in Britain. At first, it was thought to be occupying an 'ecological vacancy'. Europe is home to the European mink, which has never lived in Britain. It was claimed that the American mink was filling this gap, being intermediate in size between the larger otter and smaller stoat. It was also seen as a replacement for the polecat, which had been exterminated over much of Britain – although polecat numbers are now increasing.

However, while a few mink would have had little effect on Britain's wildlife, tens of thousands of this carnivorous animal resulted in the destruction of large numbers of other animals.

▲ *All wild mink in Britain are descended from animals that escaped from fur farms. Today, a few are still born with the silver-blue or pale brown fur that was developed in captivity. These individuals are known as pastel mink.*

Hunting high and low

Mink always remain close to water and frequent places with ample waterside vegetation. Even when roaming, they tend to follow streams and ditches. Mink eat a varied carnivorous diet, taking whatever prey is available to them on land and in water.

Mink got into zoos and parks with captive ducks – often with clipped wings so that they could not fly – and killed many birds. They also created havoc on chicken and fish farms, where they found plenty to eat but carried on killing even when they were no longer hungry. Gamekeepers soon added mink to their list of vermin.

MINK AND OTHER WILDLIFE

Soon public opinion began to swing against the mink as an unwelcome addition to British wildlife and it was blamed for ousting another fish-eating animal, the otter. However, studies show that there is little competition between these animals for food – mink eat fish that are too small for otters to bother with, and many other types of prey that are unimportant to otters. Recent research suggests that otters have had a direct impact on the far smaller mink by driving them away and sometimes even killing

◄ *The mink has a distinctive pale patch of fur stretching from its chin to its throat. It prefers its bankside territory to have wooded areas, where it can find nesting sites and extra food.*

them. Where otters are increasing, mink numbers tend to decline – dramatically so where otters have been reintroduced and their densities are particularly high.

Mink have had a severe effect on water vole populations, though. Water voles, like mink, live alongside rivers and lakes, but they are slow swimmers and easy for mink to catch in the water. Once mink occupy a new area, water vole numbers soon decline. However, although the water vole is no longer present in more than 80 per cent of the sites it inhabited before the arrival of mink, other reasons have contributed to its

▲ *A splashing doggy-paddle allows the mink to cross rivers, but to catch prey it must swim quietly underwater. A layer of dense underfur protects it against cold water in winter. Mink may even swim beneath ice.*

decline – particularly destruction of the river banks where it lives. This is now being rectified and water voles are being reintroduced to some areas.

Other inhabitants of the waterside, such as moorhens and coots, are also easily captured by mink, and in some places it has significantly reduced numbers of ducks and other waterfowl.

Freeing captive mink

In 1998, animal rights supporters broke into a number of fur farms and released several thousand mink into the wild. This act was widely condemned by conservationists and animal-welfare groups for two main reasons. Firstly, the released mink posed a serious threat to many other animals. For example, one of the fur-farm releases was in the New Forest. Here, rare reptiles and ground-nesting birds, such as the nightjar, were put at risk from the high numbers of mink set loose into the countryside. Under the Wildlife and Countryside Act,

it is illegal to release into the wild animals that have not previously occupied an area due to the damage they are likely to do. This is especially true when large numbers are released into a single area.

Secondly, such releases are cruel to the mink themselves. The animals that originally escaped to form the population of wild mink in Britain were adventurous and adaptable creatures. However, many of the released mink had never been outside a cage before and were confused and disoriented.

While some individuals no doubt learned to survive, many were easily recaptured, having never learnt the skills required to live independently of human beings. In a short time, large numbers were run over on the roads while others were killed by dogs or shot by landowners and gamekeepers. Some of the mink even found their way into people's houses, having been driven by hunger to enter via cat flaps in search of food. The majority of these freed mink were not able to fend for themselves in the wild.

▲ *As a territorial animal, the male mink will not tolerate the proximity of a rival, although it is less aggressive towards females. Male and female territories are mainly separate, but occasionally overlap.*

ISLAND INVADER

Strong swimmers, mink can easily get to small islands where birds nest out of the reach of foxes, cats and stoats. Colonies of gulls, terns and waders have been severely affected by mink invading their previously secure homes. In the sheltered waters of Scottish lochs, mink can swim as far as islands more than 3km (1¼ miles) offshore. There they may kill hundreds of adult birds and growing chicks, as well as eating the eggs. Entire colonies of seabirds have been destroyed in the space of just a few breeding seasons. In some parts of western Scotland, seabird numbers have been halved by mink.

These areas previously offered seabirds a haven in which they became particularly numerous, so it might be argued that the mink has

only reduced their numbers to a more 'natural' level. Whatever opinions might be held about the mink, it is here to stay. No amount of shooting and trapping is likely to eradicate it now. This successful predator has become an established part of Britain's wetlands.

SOLITARY HUNTER

Much smaller than the otter, mink are about 35cm (14in) long with a bushy tail. Their distinctive silky fur is much darker than that of the otter. When wet, they appear almost black whereas otters are clearly brown. The mink's droppings, which are deposited on rocks and logs at the water's edge, are easily recognisable, being thin, black and cylindrical. They smell acrid, while those of the otter have a musky but not unpleasant odour.

Mink most often live near slow-flowing rivers and lowland lakes and are less common in upland areas. In some places, particularly in Scotland, they live along the seashore. They

have formed colonies in some coastal areas where there may be as many as two mink per kilometre (just over half a mile) of rocky coast. Along the seashore, mink behave in a similar way to coastal otters, feeding on rock-pool fish, but they also climb steep, grassy cliff slopes to raid birds' nests. They are particularly partial to the eggs of gulls and terns, which are narrower at one end and therefore easy to break into. Before breaking larger eggs, a mink may drag them to cover among long vegetation. If there is an excess of food, it is often stored to eat later.

Mink are not sociable and each one tends to live in its own waterside territory, which is usually about 2–3km (1¼–1¾ miles) but sometimes as much as 6km (3⅗ miles) long. Along rivers and shores, mink territories are mainly linear, although they are more irregular around marshland. Male territories do not overlap, but often include parts of the territories of one or more females.

COURTSHIP AND BREEDING

In spring, some males set out on long journeys in search of females and may travel many kilometres across the countryside, even away from rivers. There is no pair bond and, after mating, the animals separate. Females produce just one litter each year, usually in late April or May. The average litter size is four to seven, although it can be as many as 10. In captivity, mink sometimes produce up to 17 youngsters.

The young spend up to two months in their mother's nest, which is usually situated in a burrow or among waterside stones or dense tree roots. They are weaned at around five to six weeks old. From June onwards the young mink learn how to forage and hunt for food with their mother. The family disperses when the youngsters are about 13 to 14 weeks old, and they then grow rapidly to reach adult size before the end of the year. They are capable of breeding during the following year, by the time they are 10 to 11 months old. Females are still able to breed when they are as much as seven years old, although most mink in the wild die within the first three years of life. The oldest wild mink on record lived for 10 years.

Young mink tend to move away from their mother's territory after August, sometimes travelling more than 10km (6 miles) to find a new place to live. Weaker individuals are driven away if they stray on to territory that has already been claimed. Most mink that die from natural causes probably do so as a result of territorial disputes with other mink – they may die of starvation as a result of being driven out of areas where prey is most abundant. Once individuals have established a territory, they tend to remain there, often for several years.

For its den, the mink may use an old rabbit burrow or a hiding place among rocks or even piles of brushwood. The den is rarely more than 10m (33ft) away from the water's edge and may sometimes have a separate entrance underwater. Each mink may use several dens at different times of the year, which are spread along its territory. Mink do not hibernate, although they become significantly less active during the cold winter months.

The mink's diet consists mainly of fish and birds as well as other small animals, although they also attack larger animals, such as rabbits. Invertebrates such as beetles and worms are takens, but generally they do not eat plants.

NATURAL SURVIVOR

Otters have been known to kill mink, but mink are capable of defending themselves against attacks by foxes or cats. Mink have little to fear from most natural predators, which is perhaps why they are often active in broad daylight, although they mainly hunt after dark.

Human beings are their only significant threat. Mink are in constant danger from gamekeepers and farmers, and several thousand are shot or trapped each year. Others may drown in traps set to catch fish. Mink hunting with hounds – trained to track only mink – began in the late 1970s, with a season lasting from April until October. However, mink hunting has been banned under the Hunting with Dogs legislation.

▼ *With a thick fur coat, the mink is well insulated against the worst of the winter weather. However, if rivers, lakes or marshes freeze, mink may be forced to travel farther afield in search of food.*

The water shrew

This busy little animal, which must consume half its body weight in food each day, spends most of its short life on the move. A resident of streams and ditches, it may announce its presence with a shrill squeak.

To see one of these frenetic little creatures scurrying about the water's edge is a treat well worth the patience required. Clear chalk streams, watercress beds and unpolluted ditches or ponds are the places where the water shrew chooses to live.

It needs to eat a large amount – half its body weight – every day, and so spends much of its time hunting in freshwater and in lush waterside vegetation. The water shrew is perfectly adapted for this amphibious lifestyle. A ridge of stiff hairs stretches along the underside of its tail, effectively broadening it into a flat rudder that enables the shrew to steer underwater. The tiny toes on its hind feet are fringed with bristly hairs which give the feet some resistance to the water, allowing the

▼ *Like other shrews, the water shrew must spend most of its short life searching for food or it will die of starvation. Its sensory whiskers and well-developed sense of smell are both used to detect prey.*

shrew to swim more efficiently than if it had smooth toes. Underwater, it is the hind feet that provide most of the propulsion, enabling the water shrew to dive to depths of 70cm (28in) or more.

As the water shrew swims, the pressure of the water around it squeezes air from its fur, leaving a trail of tiny silvery bubbles. Some bubbles remain on the fur, and glisten like a silvery coating over its body. The air makes the shrew buoyant, so diving is hard work – if it stops paddling with its hind feet, it immediately bobs back to the surface like a cork. To stay submerged, the shrew may lodge itself temporarily against a small stone or grip on to some underwater vegetation while seeking out its prey.

Water shrews are reliant on freshwater for their food, but nevertheless they do stray some distance from streams and ponds. They have been found in woodlands, hedgerows and on chalk downland, up to a few miles from the nearest body of freshwater. They have also occasionally been reported living on coastal beaches in Scotland, where they probably feed on sandhoppers and other small seashore creatures among the boulders above the high watermark.

DISTRIBUTION

The water shrew is found all over mainland Britain, right to the north of Scotland, but there are large gaps in its coverage. In some cases, areas measuring tens of square miles have never had a reported sighting.

▲ *In its endless quest for food, a water shrew tackles almost any very small animal it comes across. Crane flies are eagerly consumed as soon as they emerge in spring and early summer.*

The water shrew is found on many islands – including Anglesey, the Isle of Wight and various Scottish islands, such as Arran, Raasay, Skye, Mull and Bute – but not on the isles of Scilly, the Channel Islands or anywhere in Ireland. It is unlikely that the water shrew reached these

Hair care

When it comes ashore after a dive, a water shrew shakes itself vigorously to get rid of the water in its coat. Then it scratches and licks its fur to comb out any matted hairs. To finish its grooming routine, the shrew squeezes down its burrow or between densely packed grass stems to smooth the fur and remove any specks of dust or debris that may be sticking to it. It is essential that the water shrew cleans its fur well as it relies on its thick coat to keep it warm and dry under water. Air is trapped between the hairs, creating an insulating layer that stops the shrew from losing body heat in the cold water; and the fur is water repellent, which helps to prevent its skin from getting wet.

offshore islands without human assistance. At some time in the past, a shrew or two was probably scooped up with bundles of animal fodder or newly cut reeds intended for thatching or bedding, and accidentally transported to an island. This seems to have happened with many small mammal species that are now to be found on offshore islands.

▼ *Sit beside a slow-flowing stream and you may be rewarded with a sighting of a water shrew, foraging busily but unobtrusively along the shallow margins.*

The water shrew is far less abundant than either the common or pygmy shrew and lives at a lower density of population compared with other small mammals. Water shrews average three individuals per hectare (2½ acres) in their most favoured habitat, watercress beds, where a maximum of about nine individuals per hectare has been recorded. This contrasts with densities of up to 100 common shrews in a typical hectare of grassland habitat, or wood mice in woodland.

Undigested remnants of water shrews turn up infrequently in owl pellets, which is a good indicator of

the creature's rarity. They form just a tiny proportion of all the small mammals caught by barn owls (almost a third of barn owl captures may be common shrews). The water shrew is also seldom caught by cats or in small mammal traps. Its apparent scarcity is all the more surprising since it is about twice the size of the common shrew. This size advantage and its poisonous saliva mean that the water shrew can capture relatively large prey. It consumes small fish and frogs that the common shrew would be unable to tackle successfully, despite being notoriously ferocious.

Venomous bite

The water shrew is able to kill surprisingly large animals, such as newts, frogs and small fish. Studies have shown that it has a poisonous component in its saliva with which it paralyses its prey.

The water shrew usually bites its victims behind the head with its sharp little teeth. The poisonous saliva enters the prey's bloodstream through the wound and circulates to the brain, nerves and muscles, stopping the victim from struggling. The poison comes from the shrew's normal saliva-producing glands under the tongue. It is not very powerful, and bites to humans are not dangerous, even if the skin is punctured. Sometimes a reddish inflammation persists for a while, but there are no other ill effects.

The water shrew is easily recognised, so it is unlikely to be overlooked or confused with the common shrew, or any other small mammal. An adult water shrew is a very handsome creature. Typically, its back is a sleek, glossy black, and it has a sharply contrasting white belly, which is often yellowish towards the middle. White eyebrows and ear tips are frequently visible. The tail is dark on top and whitish below. There is a good deal of variation within this pattern, and all-black individuals are more common in this species than in other shrews.

DIETARY HABITS

The water shrew is active all year round, but harsh winters take their toll. When water around the edges of streams and ponds freezes solid for days or even weeks, the shrew is prevented from diving for food, and starvation becomes a real threat. Shrews usually catch half their food on the stream bed.

Water slaters, freshwater shrimps, small snails and the aquatic larvae of insects, such as caddis flies and damselflies, are the shrew's underwater prey. Their small, red-tipped teeth are sharp and well adapted for seizing and chewing up active prey including brittle-shelled

crustaceans, molluscs and insects. The iron deposits in the enamel of the red tips probably increase their resistance to wear.

The water shrew thrusts its long snout under pebbles and into tangles of vegetation in search of food. In dark water, its hunt is aided by long, sensitive whiskers on its snout. Larger prey is often brought ashore to favoured feeding sites on the banks or rocks nearby. Keen-eyed observers may notice telltale piles of remains, such as caddis fly cases and snail shells, at the water's edge.

Unsurprisingly, the water shrew's black droppings contain the remains of such aquatic prey. With the help of a microscope or a powerful magnifying glass, it is possible to identify the finely chewed fragments and distinguish them from the droppings of common shrews.

TERRITORIAL INSTINCT

Water shrews live in small burrows, about 2cm (¾in) in diameter. They sometimes adopt tunnels dug by moles and bank voles. The network of burrows includes small nesting chambers, in which dry grass and sometimes leaves are gathered to form bedding. Here, the resident shrew may spend several hours a day asleep. It also probably takes naps

elsewhere in its burrow system or in the runways it has forged through the surrounding vegetation.

Little is known about the everyday life of the water shrew, apart from the fact that it is mainly active under cover of darkness – although occasionally a shrew may be seen foraging for brief periods during the day. Water shrews often live in close proximity to one another, but they are solitary creatures and each individual keeps to itself, with adjacent home ranges overlapping very little.

Water shrews do not range widely, usually travelling no farther than 50m (55yd) from their nests. Home territories are small, perhaps 20–50 square metres (215–540sq ft) of land, with a similar area of water. Their well-developed scent glands and behaviour in captivity suggest that they are territorial animals. They mark out their ranges with small piles of droppings left on top of logs or stones to warn off intruders.

During the summer, water shrews may move about more, sometimes making excursions of up to 200m (220yd). Occasionally, they pack up and move to another location entirely. Individuals forced to move when streams dry up in summer

◀ *For much of the year, water shrews look sleek and pied in appearance. During the spring moult, however, the fur can turn brown all over, with little contrast between the upper and lower parts.*

helpless. By the fourth day, they begin to darken in colour, and by about the tenth day fur has started to grow. The family leaves the nest after about three weeks, often travelling in single file, the mother leading the way and each youngster holding on to the rump of the one in front.

The young stay close to their mother until they disperse when they are about six weeks old. Their mother may then have another litter that summer; sometimes there may even be time for a third before the season ends. This is unusual, however. Breeding is such a demanding activity that many adult females die at this time. Litters born late in the summer are generally smaller than those produced earlier in the year.

might account for some of the recorded sightings of water shrews in places well away from water.

MEETING TO MATE

Water shrews may be solitary animals, but they must meet once a year to mate. Breeding begins in April, and gestation lasts from two to three weeks. The average litter comprises six young, but sometimes ten or more babies are born. The female has five pairs of teats from which her young can suckle, two more pairs than the common shrew. Even so, large litters are unlikely to survive long in the wild.

The babies weigh just about one gram (a tiny fraction of an ounce) at birth and are blind, pink and

BRIEF LIVES

Some females may have their first litter in the same year as they themselves were born but most do not breed until the following year,

Underwater exploration

The water shrew spends much of its time hunting for prey in water. It dives in the shallows of ponds and streams for prolonged periods, although it does have to return to the surface frequently to breathe.

when they are nearly one year old. Water shrews may survive into a second winter, living for 18 or 19 months, although this is unusual. Nevertheless, water shrews live longer than common shrews, which have a maximum life span of around 14 months.

In winter, most of the water shrew population consists of growing juveniles. Many youngsters die in the first few months of independence; if they reach their first winter, they will probably survive long enough to breed.

Most water shrews die from exhaustion. The strong-smelling skin glands that all shrews possess make them unattractive prey to mammalian predators. As a result, water shrews are usually left alone and rarely eaten even when captured. Birds have a poorly developed sense of taste and are less bothered by foul odours, but nevertheless water shrews are not often eaten by owls or kestrels.

▶ *Underwater, tiny air bubbles trapped in the water shrew's fur give it a silvery appearance. This sometimes makes a shrew visible in a clear stream.*

The grey seal

When these marine mammals gather on shore to breed, they can often be seen in their hundreds at favoured sites, especially around the Scottish islands. Aggressive males vigorously defend their harem against all comers.

Two-thirds of the world's population of grey seals live around the coast of the British Isles. They spend most of their lives at sea, preferring clear, unpolluted water, but they may be seen every autumn, hauling themselves ashore to breed. They come ashore again for a short while in winter and spring to moult, and in summer they occasionally bask on rocks, resting in the warm sunshine.

Grey seal adults are around 2m (6½ft) long and the male has a horse-like face with a flat forehead that tapers into a long muzzle. The common – or harbour – seal, by contrast, has a rounded head with a small, neat muzzle, and is about half the size. While common seals are fairly evenly distributed around most of the coastline, grey seals are more abundant on northern and western shores.

BREEDING SEASON

Grey seals usually come ashore to breed in late September, but it can be as late as November in the Farne Islands, off the coast of Northumberland. They return to traditional breeding grounds, year after year, mainly on remote islands free from disturbance and predators. Mature animals return to beaches where they have successfully raised pups in the past. The oldest females arrive first and their pups, conceived in the previous season's mating, are born soon afterwards.

After giving birth to a single pup each, the females are soon ready to mate again and the adult males start to come ashore. The biggest bulls arrive first, gathering a small cluster of females and defending them against the attentions of rival males. There is no physically defined

▼ *A grey seal cow gives birth to one pup a year for up to 35 years. The females can live until the age of 45 or more.*

Threat display

Each huge bull tries to keep other males away from his own group of cows, fiercely defending his harem, which may number up to ten females. If the beach is not easily accessible, a bull may be able to occupy a strategic position and block others from coming ashore to compete for his females. In such a situation, his harem may be larger than that of other males on more open beaches.

Rival males will be chased away with a noisy display or even active combat. Some of the oldest animals bear many scars around their shoulders as souvenirs of previous encounters, but their skin is specially thickened in such areas so the wounds are superficial.

territory; the area dominated by each bull changes from day to day. Bulls proclaim their status with loud, bellowing roars, warning off rivals, and each bull fiercely chases away potential challengers. Nevertheless, sometimes fighting ensues.

The whole point of this strenuous activity is for each bull to mate with as many cows as he can in order to father as many pups as possible to carry on his genes. The bull's success depends very much on his size and stamina. Unsuccessful males will be banished to the periphery of the colony or be obliged to stay in the shallows.

The earliest bulls ashore benefit from the dominance this first claim affords them, but it comes at a price. During the breeding period, the bull does not leave his station for fear of being superseded by a rival, enduring up to eight weeks of constant alertness night and day, without going to sea to feed. The earliest bulls to arrive on the beach therefore lose the greatest amount of weight, which takes a heavy toll on their condition.

TOUGH LIFE

Survival rates are similar for both sexes up until breeding age, which starts at four to five years for cows and seven to ten years for bulls. After

that, however, the males become increasingly worn out with each successive breeding season and their life expectancy is sharply reduced – the larger the number of females and greater breeding success, the shorter the bull's life span may be. As a consequence, bull seals rarely live beyond around 20 to 25 years, whereas the cows can still be breeding ten years later.

BABY SEALS

The young are born weighing about 14kg (31lb), with a thick coat of white fur to protect them from the wind and rain. They cannot swim in this baby coat, so do not enter the water until they have moulted, revealing the adult coat underneath. This consists of special short, stiff hairs that protect the skin from being damaged as the animal heaves itself over rocks.

Insulation is provided by a thick layer of fat under the skin. This builds up rapidly as the pup grows, nourished by its mother's milk. The pup suckles every five hours or so for the first three weeks of its life. After that, the gap increases and the cow is able to return to sea to feed.

Curiously, on her return from these forays, she may sometimes feed a pup other than her own. This is presumably by mistake because the

females can ill-afford to waste precious milk on the offspring of others. The milk is formed from the mother's own fat reserves, and she loses an average of 3kg (6½lb) of body weight per day during the suckling period.

Seals produce very creamy milk which is extraordinarily rich in fat (about 55 per cent), assisting the baby to develop its own insulation and also enabling its rapid growth – the pup triples its birthweight in the first three weeks. This phenomenal weight gain is brought about solely by its mother's nutritious milk.

The mothers do little for their pups except feed them and keep away other seals that might be a nuisance. Towards the end of the suckling period, the cows mate with one or

Seal numbers

The grey seal is about three times more abundant in the British Isles than the common or harbour seal, despite the grey seal being much scarcer globally. Around 90 per cent of the British grey seal population is found in Scotland, and approximately 13,000 occur around the coasts of England and Wales.

▲ *Sea water does not normally freeze around Britain. However, in estuaries where the salt water is more dilute, it can freeze on the seal's whiskers during extremely cold weather.*

▼ *The grey seal lives at relatively high latitudes where little sunlight penetrates the water, so it needs big eyes to see in the gloomy conditions.*

more bulls and then return to the sea. This terminates family life rather suddenly and the pups are abandoned on the open beach. They go to sea for the first time shortly after this and, at around eight weeks old, must quickly learn to fend for themselves.

FISH EATERS

The grey seal's diet is almost entirely made up of fish. An adult takes around 5kg (11lb) per day of the species that are most abundant. This has brought them into conflict with fishermen in some places, such as the Orkney Isles, where they were believed to be responsible for a decline in commercial fish stocks. However, seals also take other, non-commercial species and the effect of their predation may actually be to increase the numbers of larger commercial fish, thereby benefiting fishermen.

DELAYED IMPLANTATION

The gestation period for grey seals lasts about seven months, but they are among a number of British mammals that have delayed implantation. This means that the fertilised egg does not develop immediately after mating. Instead, it enters into a state of suspended development, only implanting into the wall of the womb after a delay of up to four months. This allows the seals to mate when they are all together on the breeding beaches but the pups are not born until eight or so months later.

It is perhaps an unusual strategy to give birth at the beginning of winter when storms lash the beach. Indeed, common seals wait until the weather is more congenial, breeding and giving birth in summer. Nevertheless, the grey seal's breeding strategy is successful. On average 75 to 85 per cent of pups normally

survive to go to sea and, overall, grey seal numbers have been steadily increasing by more than 5 per cent per year in some areas.

OVERCROWDING PROBLEMS

One effect of this increase is that seals returning to the same beaches each year have found themselves having to share with ever increasing numbers. This overcrowding has forced some seals to move away from the shore, even on to rocky hillsides up to 80m (260ft) above the sea. Getting to such a height must be a huge effort for these large animals, which otherwise do not move more than a couple of metres from the water's edge.

Some of these hillside sites are far from ideal. The slopes are often covered with soil and when this is churned up by the seals in the autumn rain, it soon turns to mud. Pups born into these messy conditions suffer a high mortality rate and as many as 40 per cent

may die. However, the same can be true of pups battered by waves on overcrowded beaches.

Seals have no major predators apart from humans, although they occasionally fall prey to killer whales. Once they leave the breeding beaches, the survival of young seals is remarkably high. About two-thirds of them survive their first year, after which more than 90 per cent survive each subsequent year.

LONG-DISTANCE SWIMMERS

Little is known about the grey seal's behaviour at sea except that they travel long distances and at remarkable speeds. For instance, a pup born on the Isle of May, north of the Farne Islands, was found in Norway just nine days later and must have made the journey at a rate of around 65km (40 miles) a day. Other pups from North Rona, an uninhabited island 130km (80 miles) north-west of Cape Wrath on the north-west Scottish mainland, have turned up in Iceland.

▲ *Grey seals prefer to give birth close to the sea, the source of their food, often among rocks and boulders. They do not build nests, and muddy or grassy areas may cause problems for newborn pups.*

Seal senses

Seals are well adapted for life in and out of water. Their eyes are able to cope with a wide range of light intensities, having retinas that function well in dimly lit conditions, such as those encountered in the sea. Their ears are also modified to work underwater, with specialised tissues in the auditory canal to adjust the pressure in the ears when diving.

The long whiskers are well supplied with nerve fibres, which indicates that they may be used to detect small movements in the water, possibly caused by prey.

CHAPTER 5 • FACTFILES

The badger

NAMES
Common name: badger
Scientific name: *Meles meles*

HABITAT
Farmland, woodlands, even suburban areas, especially where there is cover among shrubs and access to good feeding areas; grasslands and cereal fields; prefers areas of well-drained soil in which to burrow, especially on slopes

STATUS
Currently estimated at just over 300,000 individuals in Britain

SIZE
Length 68–80cm (27–32in), tail 15cm (6in), ear 3cm (1¼in); weight 8–14kg (18–31lb). Females generally about 10% smaller

FEATURES
Shaggy, coarse grey fur, striped face and black belly

HABITS
Nocturnal; occupies clan territories within which members of other social groups are unwelcome; often inactive for long periods in winter, but do not hibernate

FOOD
Earthworms, beetles, wasps and other insects, small mammals, birds' eggs, roots, fruits, cereal crops and a wide range of other food

BREEDING
1–5 cubs born January–April, peaking in February. Cubs emerge above ground at about 8 weeks old

YOUNG
Similar to adults but smaller, with a shorter snout

SIGNS
Droppings often soft and deposited in small pits; distinctive hairs caught on fence wires; characteristic footprints in mud; setts with many large entrances, 20–30cm (8–12in) or more in diameter

DISTRIBUTION
Throughout mainland Britain and Ireland, except in parts of northern Scotland; scarce in lowland areas of Lancashire and East Anglia, absent from Isle of Man and most Scottish islands, but present on the Isle of Wight and Anglesey

present all year round
not present

Where to see badgers

• The most successful way to see badgers is to wait quietly outside a sett at dusk. In May the cubs often spend time playing at the entrance before moving off to feed. However, badgers are more likely to be attracted to food left by humans in late summer, when the weather is dry and the worms have burrowed deep underground.

• Many wildlife trusts and some gardens and nature reserves hold badger watch evenings. Some sites even have special hides from which to watch in comfort.

• Some farm guest houses offer badger-watching breaks, including College Barn Farm, Banbury, Oxfordshire OX15 5RY. Telephone 01295 780352 www.badger-watch.com

• Few zoos keep badgers – they spend all day asleep – but the British Wildlife Centre in Lingfield, Surrey (telephone 01342 834658) and Secret World near Bridgwater, Somerset (telephone 01278 783250) may have rescued animals. Facilities to watch them include CCTV. They are open at selected times only.

• More information and details of your local badger group are available from the National Federation of Badger Groups, 2B Inworth Street, London SW11 3EP. Telephone 020 7228 6444 www.badger.org.uk

• PROTECTED SPECIES
Badgers are fully protected by the Badgers Act of 1973 plus the Wildlife and Countryside Act 1981. Separate legislation passed in1985 protects setts. It is illegal to catch badgers, kill them, allow dogs to worry them, keep them as pets or obstruct their burrows.

The brown hare

NAMES
Common name: brown hare, European hare, common hare
Scientific name: *Lepus europaeus*

HABITAT
Mostly open farmland, especially rolling grasslands and cereal fields; sometimes small fields, open downland and even shingle or sand dunes; may use woodlands or shelter belts for lying up during the day, especially in winter

STATUS
Probably fewer than 800,000 in Britain; nationally, less common than in the recent past, but still abundant in some parts of the country; sometimes regarded as a pest

SIZE
Head and body length 55cm (22in), tail 10cm (4in), ears 10cm (4in); weight, male 3–5kg (6½–11lb), female 3–7kg (6½–15½lb)

FEATURES
Long body, powerful hind legs and large ears; tawny to russet coat with white on underparts

HABITS
Hares normally live alone, but when feeding they tend to gather in groups

FOOD
Prefers grass, wild flowers and herbs; also eats crops (especially growing cereals), sometimes bark of young trees and shrubs, especially when snow, or use of herbicides, prevents access to other food

BREEDING
Up to 3 or 4 litters per year, produced from February until October; 1–4 young per litter

YOUNG
Juveniles are similar to adults, but often have darker fur

SIGNS
Forms and trails in crops may be visible; droppings resemble large rabbit pellets but are typically paler and more fibrous

DISTRIBUTION
Throughout mainland Britain, except the north-west of Scotland; also present on Orkney, Anglesey, Isle of Wight, Isle of Man and some smaller islands; some also introduced to Ireland

present all year round
not present

Where to see brown hares

• Hares are most likely to be seen in open, rolling fields. They do not hibernate and are active all year, but they are easiest to spot in winter before grass and crops grow tall enough to hide them. From late January, the hares are increasingly active as the breeding season gets under way, but by about April they are more difficult to see in the developing cereal crops and lengthening grass.

• Unless an area is known to hold hares, watching for them is unlikely to be successful. Ask locally to discover places in which hares have been previously seen. The best times of the day to look for them are early in the morning or in the evening. Watching from a silent, motionless car may provide excellent views of hares as they forage unaware of human presence.

The common dormouse

NAMES
Common name: common dormouse, hazel dormouse
Scientific name: *Muscardinus avellanarius*

HABITAT
Mixed deciduous woodland, copses, hedgerows where a variety of berry and seed-bearing trees and shrubs occur, especially hazel and honeysuckle; thrives in sunny, dry conditions

STATUS
Probably 45,000 individuals in England and Wales

SIZE
Head and body length 60–90mm (2⅜–3½in), tail length 55–70mm (2¼–2¾in); weight 15–40g (½–1½oz)

FEATURES
Bushy tail, bright orange-brown or reddish fur, large black eyes, short muzzle and long whiskers

HABITS
Nocturnal and arboreal, emerging at night to clamber through vegetation in search of food. Returns to nest before dawn and spends eight hours in normal sleep. Hibernates for 5–6 months each year in small nest on woodland floor

FOOD
Nuts, especially hazel and beech; seeds, berries, pollen, nectar-bearing plants and insects

BREEDING
2–7 young, usually born July–August after gestation of 3½ weeks; occasional second litter in early autumn

NEST
Compact, tightly woven ball of shredded honeysuckle bark and leaves; in summer, sometimes built in old bird's nest or squirrel's drey; in winter, on woodland floor among leaf litter; readily uses nesting boxes

YOUNG
Born blind and naked; fur grows at about 1 week old and is greyer than adult's

DISTRIBUTION
Scattered populations in England and Wales as far north as Northumberland

present all year round
not present

Where to see common dormice

• Copses that are linked to larger woodlands by a network of hedgerows and corridors of uncultivated land are excellent places to look for dormice. Very small copses and short stretches of hedgerow are not suitable because they do not contain enough food for dormice and all the other small mammals with which they compete.

• If work is being carried out in a wood, a dormouse may be disturbed. In this case, it will always rush upwards, climbing towards the tree canopy.

• In summer, look out for cream and yellow flowers of honeysuckle scattered on the ground under hedgerows. Dormice pull the flowers off the shoots before they have been pollinated so that they can eat the sugary nectar.

• In autumn, look for nibbled hazel nut shells. Dormice eat the nuts where they find them and drop the shells to the ground.

• Most wildlife trusts in southern England now have at least one reserve where dormice are a special feature. For further information contact the Mammal Society at 2B Inworth Street, London SW11 3EP (telephone 020 7350 2200) or visit www.abdn.ac.uk/mammal

• PROTECTED SPECIES
Under the provisions of the Wildlife and Countryside Act, 1986, it is illegal to kill or injure a common dormouse, or to disturb it in its nest.

The common shrew

NAMES
Common name: common shrew
Scientific name: *Sorex araneus*

HABITAT
Woodland, farmland and hedgerow

STATUS
Nearly 42 million individuals; population peaks in summer

SIZE
Head and body length 50–80mm (2–3¼in), tail length 30–50mm (1¼–2in); weight 5–12g (¼–½oz)

FEATURES
Very small, brown all over with lighter brown flanks and pale belly; long, pointed nose, small ears, tiny eyes

HABITS
Active day and night in long grass, under shrubs and below ground; frequent short periods of rest

FOOD
Largely invertebrates, especially earthworms, slugs, snails, insect larvae and beetles; occasionally vertebrates

BREEDING
Usual litter 6 or 7, but sometimes as many as 10; 2 litters per season (rarely 3 or 4), born April–September

NEST
A ball of interwoven dried grass and small leaves, constructed under logs, grass tussocks or in burrows of other species

YOUNG
Paler brown than adult with less sharp demarcation between upper and undersides; tail covered with short bristly hair

SIGNS
Visual signs are too small to notice, but loud squeaks of aggression or fear are frequently heard

DISTRIBUTION
Throughout mainland Britain and on many offshore islands, but absent from Ireland, the Scilly Isles and the Channel Islands; tends to be less abundant at high altitudes

■ present all year round
□ not present

Where to see common shrews

• Common shrews live in woodland, farmland and hedgerows but tend to stay under cover to avoid predators. Nevertheless, owls do catch and eat shrews, and their skulls can be seen in owl pellets. The skulls are narrow and pointed, with red tips on all the teeth.

• Shrews can be detected by the high-pitched squeals they make when confronting other shrews.

• Shrews are often found dead on footpaths where they have been dropped by predators that do not find their taste palatable.

• PROTECTED SPECIES
All shrews are given partial protection by the Wildlife and Countryside Act, 1981. They may not be deliberately trapped or killed without a special licence.

The fallow deer

NAMES
Common name: fallow deer
Scientific name: *Dama dama*

HABITAT
Woodland, farmland and deer parks, with dense undergrowth in places; often semi-domesticated

STATUS
Around 100,000 individuals at start of breeding season. Common within its range, absent in other areas except for the occasional stray or escaped animal

SIZE
Length 160cm (5ft 3in); tail 20cm (8in); height about 85cm (33½in) at the shoulder; male weight about 70kg (155lb), female weight just over half this total

FEATURES
Flat antlers unique among British deer; colour varies from white to almost black, but typically rich brown with white spots, brightest and most boldly spotted in summer and autumn; tail usually black on top, surrounded by white patch edged with black

HABITS
Feed by grazing grass or browsing trees and bushes; often active mainly at night, especially on farmland; may spend the day hidden among trees or shrubs

BREEDING
Bucks gather harems of does in autumn, mate in October; fawns born singly in June – twins rare

NEST
Deer make no nest, but hide young among long grass, bracken or weeds

YOUNG
Usually pale brown, spotted with white; lie hidden for a few days before following at mother's heels

DISTRIBUTION
Most of southern and central England; parts of Wales, northern England and Ireland, and a few scattered localities in Scotland

present all year round
not present

Where to see fallow deer

• There are many deer parks all over the country where fallow deer (and in some cases other species as well) can be seen. Good examples are:

• Richmond Park, Surrey

• Charlecote Park, Stratford-upon-Avon, Warwickshire

• Powderham Park, near Exeter, Devon

• Studley Royal Park, near Ripon, Yorkshire

• The Scottish Deer Park, Cupar, Fife

• For more information about deer, and to find out about deer in your area, contact the British Deer Society, The Walled Garden, Burgate Manor, Fordingbridge, Hampshire SP6 1EF. Telephone 01425 655433 www.bds.org.uk

• PROTECTED SPECIES
Fallow deer are protected by legislation that controls hunting: they may not be killed at certain times of the year. Various laws regulate methods of capture, types of weapons that can be used to cull them, and how they may be moved around.

The field vole

NAMES
Common name: field vole,
short-tailed vole
Scientific name: *Microtus agrestis*

HABITAT
Thick grassland, moorland, sand dunes,
young conifer plantations and sometimes
hedgerows and open woodland

STATUS
Abundant where it occurs, but patchy
in the lowlands; estimated 75 million
individuals at the start of the breeding
season

SIZE
Head and body length 80–135mm
(3⅛–5⅜in), tail length 18–50mm
(¾–2in); weight 15–50g (½–1½oz)

FEATURES
Normally greyish brown above, with grey
belly; tail uniform pinkish brown and
short, less than one-third length of head
and body; face typically blunt-nosed, with
small eyes and ears barely projecting
beyond the fur; often squeaks if alarmed
or handled; has a distinctive musky,
cheesy smell

HABITS
Mainly nocturnal, but often active during
the day; adults compete for territory and
are quick to fight

FOOD
Mostly grass, also other plant material,
including clover, young bark and bulbs

BREEDING
Up to 7 litters of 4–6 young produced
March–October; gestation period
18–20 days

NEST
Ball of finely shredded grass, about 10cm
(4in) in diameter, situated underground or
among grass roots

YOUNG
Born pink and blind, weighing 2g (fraction
of an ounce); weaned at 2 weeks

SIGNS
Small piles of oval, green droppings
about 3–4mm (⅛in) long, and tiny heaps
of shredded and chewed grass, left in
tunnels among grass tussocks

DISTRIBUTION
Throughout mainland Britain and on some
islands; absent from Ireland and many
Scottish islands, the Isles of Man, Scilly
and Lundy, and the Channel Islands

present all year round
not present

Where to see field voles

• The field vole's world is normally
invisible, buried deep among dense
masses of old grass. Pulling apart grass
tussocks may expose vole tunnels among
the stem bases and roots. Piles of
nibbled grass or oval green droppings
are evidence of field voles.

• Sheets of corrugated iron or
hardboard lying in grass offer shelter
under which field voles like to build
their nests. These are made of finely
shredded grass, with tunnels leading off
in different directions, and may be
clearly visible if the sheet is lifted. Do
not expose the nest for long and always
replace the sheet carefully.

• Sometimes in winter, all may be
revealed when snow melts after it has
been lying on the ground for a long
time. While the snow is present, the
voles make new runs on top of the
grass, but hidden under the snow. When
the snow melts, masses of runs, burrows
and nests are suddenly exposed.

The fox

NAMES
Common name: fox, red fox
Scientific name: *Vulpes vulpes*

HABITAT
From fields to mountains, farms to
woodland, sand dunes to city centres

STATUS
Probably more than 250,000 and may
be increasing; often regarded as a pest

SIZE
Body 60–70cm (2ft–2ft 4in), tail 40cm
(16in); adult body weight male 6–7kg
(13¼–15½lb), female 10% smaller

FEATURES
Orange-brown body, white throat, long
bushy tail that often has a white tip;
prominent ears 9cm (3½in) long, with
black outer surface

HABITS
Lives alone or in small family group

FOOD
Rabbits, mice and other small mammals,
birds, earthworms and beetles; also
scavenged carcasses, fruit, fish, eggs
and a large range of other foods

BREEDING
Mates from late December to early
February; 4–5 young born in March

EARTH
Uses existing burrows or digs its own;
may make temporary nest above ground
or live under a garden shed.

YOUNG
Born covered with dark, chocolate-
brown, velvety fur, blind and deaf – eyes
open at 11–14 days, milky looking at
first, blue until 1 month old; juveniles
are similar to adults, but have less
bushy tails

SIGNS
Earth entrance holes about 20cm (8in)
in diameter, but long-established ones
are much larger with a fan of dug-out
soil in front; grey twisted droppings
containing fur and bone fragments; very
distinctive fox smell, pungent and acrid –
quite different from that of a dog – can
often be smelt on the wind, around
burrows or near food and droppings

DISTRIBUTION
Throughout Britain and Ireland,
except the Isle of Man and some
Scottish islands

■ present all year round
☐ not present

Where to see foxes

• Foxes are more likely to be seen in
towns and cities than in the country.

• At dusk and after dark, foxes
come out in search of food, especially
in parks and gardens and on waste
ground.

• In safe, quiet places, they may be
seen basking in the sunshine.

• Foxes often inhabit railway
embankments and may be seen
from trains.

The grey seal

NAMES
Common name: grey seal, Atlantic seal; male is a bull, female a cow
Scientific name: *Halichoerus grypus*

HABITAT
Rocky coasts, especially uninhabited islands and isolated beaches with sea caves

STATUS
More than 130,000

SIZE
Bulls about 2m (6½ft) long, cows 1.8m (6ft); weight 150–250kg (331–551lb); bull is about 50% heavier than female

FEATURES
Flat forehead and elongated snout; bulls usually dark grey with a few pale patches; cows more variable but generally lighter with pale cream on belly and scattering of dark blotches all over

HABITS
Largely inactive when ashore; at sea, sometimes seen 'bottling' – floating upright in the water with just nostrils above the surface; when feeding, spend 80% of time under water

FOOD
Mainly fish from a wide range of species; also crustaceans, squid, octopus and occasionally seabirds

BREEDING
Single pup born late autumn

NEST
No nest; females give birth among rocks and stones, or on sandy beach; occasionally on hillside

YOUNG
Born with thick, white coat; moult to pale grey before going to sea for first time at 8 weeks old

SIGNS
Large brown or grey droppings (often containing fish bones) left on rocks; droppings are bright orange during breeding season

DISTRIBUTION
Mostly around western and northern Scotland, but also Farne Islands and other undisturbed breeding grounds

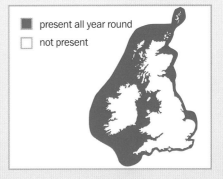

present all year round

not present

Where to see grey seals

• The best place to see grey seals is the Farne Islands off the coast of Northumberland. Boat trips go from the town of Seahouses in the summer.

• Up to 1000 grey and common seals can be seen off Tentsmuir Beach, Newport on Tay, near St Andrews. Other Scottish seal resorts include Loch Linnhe (boat trips from Fort William), the Isle of Skye, Shetland, Orkney and several places along the Cape Wrath to John O'Groats road.

• Boats visit Hilbre Island from Thurstaston in the Wirral, Cheshire. Seal watching boat trips are available from various places around Cornwall.

• One of the largest colonies is on the Isle of May in the Firth of Forth.

• Strumble Head in Pembrokeshire offers views of grey seals and pups.

• PROTECTED SPECIES
Grey seals have been legally protected by their own separate Act of Parliament since 1914. They may not be killed around British coasts between 1 September and 31 December without a licence. The last organised cull in the UK was in 1983.

The grey squirrel

NAMES
Common name: grey squirrel
Scientific name: *Sciurus carolinensis*

HABITAT
Deciduous woodland, parks, gardens, hedgerows; urban areas with trees

STATUS
An estimated 2.5 million individuals in Britain; unknown but increasing number in Ireland

SIZE
Length 24–28cm (9½–11in),tail 19–24cm (7½–9½in); weight 400–600g (14–21oz), pregnant female heavier

FEATURES
Grey fur on neck, back and tail; underside creamy white; flanks and feet sometimes reddish in summer; tail has a white fringe (each hair is banded brown and black with a white tip)

HABITS
Active in daylight, on ground and up trees

FOOD
Buds, flowers, fruits, nuts, fungi, tree bark; occasional birds' eggs and nestlings

BREEDING
Mating chases in late winter; 1 or 2 litters of 1–6 young (usually 3, occasionally 7) produced February–July; in the south of England, young may be born as early as January and as late as September

NEST
Called a drey, about the size of a football; made of twigs with leaves still attached; built in trees and tall bushes

YOUNG
Born naked and blind; fur grows in 2–3 weeks, eyes open in 4 weeks; independent in 2½–4 months; resemble adult but tail less bushy

DISTRIBUTION
Throughout most of England and Wales; central Scotland; parts of Ireland

present all year round

not present

Where to see grey squirrels

• Grey squirrels are common in many parts of the country. The best places to observe them closely are city parks where the animals can become very tame and will often take food from the hand.

• Early in the morning is a good time to see them. The squirrels are hungry and go out foraging before disturbance levels rise during the day.

• Grey squirrels are often attracted to garden bird tables and birdfeeders, where they display considerable agility and ingenuity to reach the food.

• PROTECTED SPECIES
The grey squirrel is not legally protected but is listed on Schedule 9 of the Wildlife and Countryside Act. This means that any squirrels that are captured (or taken into care because they are injured, for instance) may not be re-released into the wild. It is also illegal to keep grey squirrels in captivity without a licence.

The harvest mouse

NAMES
Common name: harvest mouse
Scientific name: *Micromys minutus*

HABITAT
Ungrazed hay meadows and other places
with tall, stiff-stemmed weeds and long
grass; hedge bases, reedbeds and edges
of cornfields

STATUS
Around 1,415,000 in England, plus
10,000 in Wales

SIZE
Head and body length 50–70mm
(2–2¾in), tail about 60mm (2⅜in);
ear about 9mm (⅜in) long; weight
of adult averages about 6g (¼oz)

FEATURES
Tiny, agile mouse; fur russet-orange, white
underside well-delineated; nose blunt;
ears small and hairy; tail tip prehensile
(adapted for gripping), a feature that is
unique among European mammals

HABITS
Climbs stems of tall grasses, reeds and
similar vegetation; in winter may descend
to ground and occupy burrows; active
mainly at night, sometimes during day,
especially in summer

FOOD
Seeds (including cereal grains), green
shoots in spring, small fruits, insects
(especially in summer)

BREEDING
Breeds from May until October, but as
late as December if weather is mild;
most litters born August–September;
average litter 6, occasionally 8 or more

NEST
Woven ball of shredded grass, about the
size of a tennis ball

YOUNG
Born naked; fine fur grows after 4 days;
eyes open after 8 or 9 days;
independent at around 14 days. Fur
distinctly greyer than adult's, otherwise
similar. Mature at 35 days

SIGNS
Distinctive spherical nests woven in tall
vegetation, otherwise easily overlooked

DISTRIBUTION
Widespread but patchy in southern and
eastern England, scarcer in the north,
especially the north-west; present in a few
areas of Wales, mainly coastal; very few in
Scotland; absent from Ireland

present all year round
not present

Where to see harvest mice

• Southern England is the best place to
look for harvest mice. The nests are far
easier to find than the actual animals.
Look in field corners with long grass –
more than knee high. Search the dead
grasses at the foot of old hedges, and
low brambles at the edge of fields with
permanent grass.

• Nests are most numerous in early
autumn when the vegetation is still
standing tall. Later when the grasses
collapse, nests are harder to find but the
harvest mice themselves may be seen as
they are forced to travel along the
ground, often in daylight. Later in the
winter, mortality will take its toll and
the animals will be fewer and seen less
often.

The hedgehog

NAMES
Common name: hedgehog
Scientific name: *Erinaceus europaeus*

HABITAT
Farmland, short-grass areas, hedges, woodlands, town parks and gardens

STATUS
Between 1 and 2 million individuals in UK. Nationally common although probably declining; may be more numerous in north-east England than elsewhere

SIZE
Length 20–30cm (8–12in); weight average 450–680g (1–1½lb), but up to 800g (2lb) before hibernation. Can reach up to 1.2kg (2½lb) in wild

FEATURES
Unmistakable due to brown spiny coat

HABITS
Mainly nocturnal, normally solitary, does not defend territory

FOOD
Beetles, worms, caterpillars, slugs and wide range of other small animals, including small mammals and nestling birds and eggs

BREEDING
Usually 4–5 (up to 7) young born mainly June–July; late litters born September to October

NEST
Constructs bed of tightly packed leaves for winter hibernation; in spring, builds similar but larger nest to give birth; in summer shelters in any long vegetation, often with no real nest, especially in warm weather

YOUNG
Born after about 40 days' gestation. Spines develop rapidly – white at first, then brown; eyes open at 14 days old. Young are independent at around six weeks

DISTRIBUTION
Throughout Britain and Ireland, including urban areas; absent from mountains and other very open places; introduced to most offshore islands – its liking for birds' eggs has made it unwelcome on some of these

present all year round
not present

Where to see hedgehogs

• In the garden, hedgehogs are best seen at night using a powerful torch. Select an area of short grass, preferably on damp soil where worms are abundant. Still, warm evenings are best.

• Look for characteristic black droppings on the lawn that show that a hedgehog has visited. The droppings are about 3cm (1in) long, crinkly, and studded with the shiny black remains of beetles.

• Outside the garden, golf courses are generally good places to see hedgehogs, except for the greens where the heavy application of chemicals removes all the hedgehog's invertebrate prey.

• Playing fields are also worth investigating. Cemeteries and places with longer grass are even more likely to have hedgehogs, but they are difficult to spot among tall vegetation.

• PROTECTED SPECIES
Hedgehogs are partially protected through the Wildlife and Countryside Act. They may not be trapped or killed without a licence. Recent anti-cruelty legislation offers protection from ill treatment, making it an offence to tease or torture wild animals.

The mink

NAMES
Common name: American mink, mink
Scientific name: *Mustela vison*

HABITAT
Mostly lowland areas, beside rivers, lakes and ponds

STATUS
Around 36,000; major decline since 1995

SIZE
Length head and body 30–45cm (12–18in), tail 13–23cm (5–9in); weight adult females about 450–800g (16–28oz), males 850–1800g (30–63½oz)

FEATURES
Coat chocolate-brown to black with pale markings on chin, throat and underside; silver-blue or pale brown mutations; feet slightly webbed

HABITS
Active day and night, but mostly in the evening and after dark; lives near water

FOOD
Fish, frogs, small mammals, waterside birds and their eggs; some invertebrates; raids fish farms and captive waterfowl

BREEDING
One litter per year, in April or May; usually 4–7 young per litter; weaning period is 5–6 weeks

NEST
Uses burrows and lairs among tree roots at water's edge, also rabbit burrows; rarely digs its own burrows

YOUNG
Resemble adult, but smaller

SIGNS
Footprints in soft mud show pad and often only 4 of the 5 toes in a splayed-out star shape, 2.5–4cm (1–1½in) long and 2–4cm (¾–1½in) wide; droppings tapered at each end, about 5–8cm (2–3in) long, typically 1cm (½in) diameter, deposited on waterside objects such as stones and logs, unpleasantly smelly

DISTRIBUTION
Almost everywhere in mainland Britain; absent from Isle of Wight, Isle of Man and Anglesey; absent from extreme north of Scotland but present on Lewis and Arran

■ present all year round
□ not present

Where to see mink

• The best places to look for mink are beside quiet, slow-flowing rivers, especially in Kent, Sussex, Devon and Pembrokeshire, where they have long been established in the wild.

• Asking local anglers where they see mink is one way to find a spot to watch for them. Another is to search under bridges and on boulders and logs for their characteristic droppings.

• Select a suitable tree or bridge as a vantage point and watch quietly without moving. The best time to look is in the early evening.

The mole

NAMES
Common name: mole (old English names are 'moldewarp' and 'want')
Scientific name: *Talpa europaea*

HABITAT
Mainly grassland and grassy areas, such as lawns; also farmland and woodland

STATUS
About 30 million individuals in Britain

SIZE
Length head and body 13–15cm (5–6in), tail 2cm (¾in); weight 70–130g (2½–4½oz), but highly variable; males usually larger than females

FEATURES
Torpedo-shaped body with black fur; front paws very big, snout and paws pink, eyes and ears inconspicuous

HABITS
Solitary; spends most of its life underground

FOOD
Mostly earthworms; also beetles, centipedes, caterpillars and other insect larvae

BREEDING
Mating only possible a few days in the year, between February and March; litter size usually 3–4; 1 litter per year

NEST
A ball of grass underground, often below an extra-large molehill, called a 'fortress'

YOUNG
Born tiny, naked and blind in April or May (later in Scotland); fur begins to grow at 14 days old; eyes open after approximately 22 days; independent 35–40 days after birth, when they leave the nest

SIGNS
Series of mounds of earth excavated while tunnelling

DISTRIBUTION
Throughout England, Wales and Scotland but scarce at high altitudes; absent from Ireland and some islands

■ present all year round
□ not present

Where to see moles

• In long periods of hot dry weather, moles find it difficult to obtain sufficient food underground, and they spend a lot more time at the surface. Go out very early in the morning after a few weeks without rain and you may hear a mole as it tears at clumps of grass in search of food. You might also be able to see one scurrying from one feeding place to another.

• If you are lucky, you might glimpse a mole as it swims across a small stream or crosses a road.

• If you watch a fresh molehill quietly, you may see it begin to move as the mole pushes up more soil from below. Your patience may be rewarded as the mole emerges onto the surface and you can get a good look at it.

The mountain hare

NAMES
Common name: mountain hare, blue hare, Irish hare, white hare
Scientific name: *Lepus timidus*

HABITAT
Heather moorland, mountain grassland, rocky hilltops

STATUS
Numbers fluctuate wildly but not endangered at national level; up to around 350,000 individuals in Scotland; unknown number in Ireland, where it is the common hare species, and a few in England

SIZE
Length about 50–55cm (20–22in), ears about 7cm (2¾in), tail about 7cm (2¾in); weight 2.5–3kg (5½–6½lb)

FEATURES
Usually occurs above 130m (425ft); dusky blue underfur on flanks; moults from brown to white (in Ireland usually only ears, feet and tail turn white) in mid-October–January, then back to brown in mid-February–late May; third moult occurs in June–September

HABITS
Mainly solitary, but feeds in groups in the open, often at night; more active in the day during mating season (February–August)

FOOD
Short young heather, bilberry, bark and twigs of gorse in winter; grasses, legumes, herbs and farm crops in summer

BREEDING
Up to 4 young per litter (largest number in cold years), 2 or 3 litters per year; young born fully furred, eyes open, weaned after 4 weeks

NEST
None, but lies up in a 'form' in long heather, made by biting through stems; may scrape a shallow burrow in snow for shelter in winter

YOUNG
Similar to adult

SIGNS
Heaps of spherical droppings; footprints indicate round forefeet and heavily furred, long hind feet; forms conspicuous, as are well-trodden, nibbled trails in heather

DISTRIBUTION
Mountainous areas in Scotland, and some islands; about 500 in England, also present on Isle of Man; all over Ireland; extinct in Wales

present all year round
not present

Where to see mountain hares

• Mountain hares can best be seen by walking on heather moors in Scotland. They are common south of Banchory, Aberdeenshire, for example, and on the Cairngorms.

• In the Peak District National Park hares can be seen in small numbers. The best time is late winter when their white fur stands out against dark moorland scenery.

• In Ireland, this species is known as the Irish hare. It can often be seen living in large groups in many farmland areas in the lowlands, in the fields around Aldergrove (Belfast) airport, for example, as well as on higher ground. Irish hares do not go completely white in winter.

Native ponies

NAMES
Common names: Dartmoor pony, Exmoor pony, New Forest pony, Dales pony, Fell pony, Highland pony, Eriskay pony, Shetland pony, Welsh Mountain pony, Connemara pony
Scientific name: *Equus caballus*

HABITAT
Moorland, mountains and forest

STATUS
Pure breeds nationally scarce, but often abundant in their native areas

SIZE
Height at shoulder: varies from Shetland pony at about 1m (3ft) to Connemara, Dales and Highland ponies up to about 1.47m (4ft 10in)

FEATURES
Sturdy and strong, with deep chest and short, strong legs; variably coloured according to breed; coat appears fine and glossy in summer, dense and hairy in winter; long tail and mane

HABITS
Sociable, living in small herds; not afraid of people or cars; active day and night

FOOD
Mainly grass; heather, moss, leaves, holly and shrubs, such as gorse and bramble, in winter

BREEDING
Mating occurs in summer; gestation averages 335 days and foals are born in the open March–September (occasionally later) the following year, most born April–May

YOUNG
Resemble adult

SIGNS
Large heaps of coarse, round faecal pellets (or droppings), each ball about 5cm (2in) in diameter; footprints semi-circular

DISTRIBUTION
Semi-wild herds in Dartmoor, Exmoor, New Forest, Welsh mountains, both sides of Pennines, Scottish Highlands and Islands, Shetland Isles and Connemara in County Galway, Ireland

■ present all year round
☐ not present

Where to see native ponies

• The open moorland of Exmoor, home to the Exmoor ponies, spans the border between Somerset and north Devon. A small herd has also been introduced to the Cumbrian hills.

• Several herds of Dartmoor ponies live on different parts of Dartmoor. They can be seen from the road from Ashburton to Tavistock and often gather near car parks.

• Shetland ponies are found in small herds on most of the Shetland islands. Those on Unst are the easiest to observe.

• Welsh Mountain ponies run wild on some Welsh hills and also in English border county areas, such as the Long Mynd in Shropshire.

• New Forest ponies range freely through the woodland and villages in the New Forest, Hampshire.

• Dales and Fell ponies roam along the eastern and western sides of the Pennines respectively.

• Connemara ponies can be found in Connemara, County Galway, in the west of Ireland.

The otter

NAMES
Common name: otter
Scientific name: *Lutra lutra*

HABITAT
Rivers, lakes and sheltered coastal areas

STATUS
Probably 7000–10,000, of which most live in Scotland

SIZE
Male length up to 90–130cm (35½–51¼in), of which about 35–45cm (14–17¾in) is tail; weight 6–15kg (14–33lb); female slightly smaller

FEATURES
Brown fur, white on face and underparts; broad, flat head, small ears; webbed feet

HABITS
Usually solitary; spends much of its time in water

FOOD
Mainly fish; also crustaceans, molluscs, insects, worms, frogs; sometimes birds and small mammals

BREEDING
Any time, but most births May–August, especially in Shetland; normally 2 or 3 cubs in a litter

NEST
May use up to 30 lairs for daytime shelter; for breeding, a holt is built above flood level

YOUNG
Born after 62 days gestation, measuring about 12cm (4⅓in) in length and weighing about 100g (3½oz); cubs swim at 3 months and leave home at around 10–12 months

SIGNS
Distinctive tar-like droppings; tracks in mud or soft sand; muddy chutes down steep banks into water; well-worn trails through vegetation from one section of river bank to another

DISTRIBUTION
Rare or absent from much of central and south-east England; small stronghold in East Anglia; widespread in south-west England, Wales, north of England, Scotland and Ireland

- present all year round
- not present

Where to see otters

- Otters are extremely shy and usually nocturnal. However, coastal otters are often active in the daytime. The best places to see otters are in Shetland and western Scotland, including the Hebridean islands, especially along quiet rocky shores and around sea lochs.

- There is an otter haven and visitors' hide at the southern end of the Isle of Skye, and otters are frequently seen on Loch Sunart and the Isle of Mull.

- The RSPB reserve at Leighton Moss in Lancashire has hides from which otters are quite often seen.

- If you locate a sprainting spot by a bridge over a river in Wales, Devon or the north of England, it is well worth spending an hour or two watching for the otter from the bridge at dawn or dusk.

- Otters are present on areas of low-lying wet fields, such as the Somerset Levels, but there are few vantage points from which to watch them and nowhere to hide.

- Some zoos keep otters in pools where you may be able to see them swimming underwater.

- PROTECTED SPECIES
The otter is afforded full legal protection under Schedule 5 of the Wildlife and Countryside Act. It is an offence to kill otters or disturb them or their nests.

The pine marten

NAMES
Common name: pine marten
Scientific name: *Martes martes*

HABITAT
Woodland with patches of open ground and grassy rides

STATUS
Rare, but increasing, at least in Scotland

SIZE
Length (head and body) 50–55cm (20–22in), tail 20–25cm (8–10in); weight (adult male) up to 1.7kg (3lb 12oz). Females about 10% smaller

FEATURES
Dark brown fur, thick bushy tail, creamy throat patch; short legs; sharp, semi-retractable claws; prominent, triangular ears about 4cm (1½in) long, with pale edges

HABITS
Mainly active at night and at dusk and dawn, but also active during daylight in summer; solitary

FOOD
Small mammals, especially voles; fruits, worms, insects, birds' eggs, fish, fruit, fungi, carrion and scraps

BREEDING
Mates July–August; young (kits) born March–April due to delayed implantation; one litter each year; 1–5 kits (average 3)

NEST
Makes dens in tree holes, rock crevices and under logs; also uses nestboxes and old squirrel nests

YOUNG
Similar to adult, but with shorter fur

SIGNS
Footprints like those of a small dog, usually paired prints; droppings long and black, usually deposited singly in conspicuous locations

DISTRIBUTION
Mainly in Scotland, with a few scattered individuals in parts of Wales and northern England; more widespread in Ireland

present all year round
not present

Where to see pine martens

• Central and western Scotland are the most likely areas to see pine martens.

• You may see one in car headlights as it sprints across the road.

• At some picnic sites pine martens have taken to searching for scraps and raiding the waste bins.

• Pine martens may feed at garden bird tables in some areas.

• Ask local people if they know where to look.

• PROTECTED SPECIES
The pine marten is a fully protected species. Partly protected by the Wildlife and Countryside Act of 1981, it was granted full protection in 1988 when the legislation was amended to include any den or other structure used by a pine marten for shelter or refuge.

The pipistrelle

NAMES
Common name: pipistrelle
Scientific name: *Pipistrellus pipistrellus; pipistrellus pygmaeus; pipistrellus nathusii*

HABITAT
Various, including parks, gardens, farmland and open woodland; prefers areas near water

STATUS
Most numerous British bat – perhaps about 2 million individuals, but probably declining in numbers overall

SIZE
Length, head and body, 35–45mm (1⅜–1¾in); wingspan 18–25cm (7–10in); weight 3.5–8.5g (⅛–¼oz)

FEATURES
Postcalcarial lobe – small bulge, about 3x2mm (⅛x¹⁄₁₆in), on outer edge of the calcar, a tiny spur that projects from the heel of the hind foot, stiffening the edge of the tail membrane

HABITS
Flies at dusk until shortly before dawn, depending on weather

FOOD
Small insects, especially midges

BREEDING
Mates in autumn, birth of single young in June–mid-July

NEST
None; roosts in crevices, especially in buildings, under tiles and behind wooden cladding

YOUNG
Resembles adult, capable of first flight at 3 weeks but remains in the nursery roost until 5 weeks old; can catch food for itself at 6 weeks, but mothers and young stay in contact for much longer

SIGNS
Very small, sticky droppings; accumulations of them may be slightly smelly if damp

DISTRIBUTION
All of mainland Britain and Ireland, and some islands

present all year round
not present

Where to see pipistrelles

• Often the first signs of pipistrelles are their tiny droppings, around 5mm (¼in) long and scarcely thicker than a piece of black thread. Slightly crinkly and irregular in shape, unlike the oval pellets of mice, they are sometimes seen sticking to walls and windows, ejected by the bats in flight or as they leave the roost. Bats eat insects, so if the droppings are crumbled and inspected with a magnifying glass, tiny bits of insect may be seen.

• Bats are harmless, but you may not like them living at close quarters. This is not, however, an excuse for killing them or blocking the roost entrance, leaving the young inside to starve to death. All bats are legally protected, even when they are living in your own house. If they cause genuine problems, you can get advice from the Bat Conservation Trust, Unit 2, 15 Cloisters House, 8 Battersea Park Road, London SW8 4BG (telephone 020 7627 2629) or visit www.bats.org.uk

• PROTECTED SPECIES
Like all other bats in the UK, pipistrelles are fully protected under the Wildlife and Countryside Act, 1981; roosts are also protected.

The rabbit

NAMES
Common name: rabbit
Scientific name: *Oryctolagus cuniculus*

HABITAT
Field edges, grasslands, farmland, open deciduous woodland, heathland, road verges and railway embankments, large gardens and allotments, sand dunes; not normally found in wet places or on high moorland

STATUS
Very abundant in places; population crashes frequent, with perhaps 70% or more dying in a short time. Most recent population estimates are in the region of 38 million individuals at start of breeding season

SIZE
Length head and body up to 400mm (16in), tail about 30mm (1¼in); adult body weight 1.2–2kg (2–4½lb); sexes similar in size

FEATURES
Grey-brown body, greyish white belly and orange-buff on the neck; big ears, up to 70mm (3in) long; hind feet 75–95mm (3–4in) long; large brown eyes; tail black on top, fluffy white below

HABITS
Normally lives in social groups, rarely far from cover or from burrow entrances; feeding and other activity mostly at night, but also often seen during the day

FOOD
Mainly grasses, crops and wild plants; leaves and young shoots of trees and tree bark, especially in winter

BREEDING
Mainly from late January to late July, peaks April–May; litters of 3–7 or more young (average 5) produced at about 5 week intervals; 4–6 litters per year

NEST
Usually in burrows, often in groups; may make a temporary nest on the surface

YOUNG
Smaller size and shorter ears than adults

SIGNS
Clusters of compact spherical droppings

DISTRIBUTION
Throughout Britain, including Ireland and most of the Scottish islands

■ present all year round
☐ not present

Where to see rabbits

• Rabbits pop up all over the place, but are often seen basking in the evening sunshine along hedges, field margins and the edges of coppices and woodland.

• Railway embankments are frequently colonised by rabbits and it's worth watching for them from passing trains.

• In parks and gardens, rabbits may become quite tame and approachable, but they are usually controlled because of the damage they do to plants.

• Look for entrances to burrows. These average about 15cm (6in) in diameter, but can be a little narrower or wider (up to about 40cm/16in).

The red deer

NAMES
Common name: red deer
Scientific name: *Cervus elaphus*

HABITAT
Forests and woods, especially conifer plantations in Scotland; open hillsides (including heather moorland) especially in Scotland and the Pennines

STATUS
Total British wild population more than 360,000 plus more than 800 in Ireland

SIZE
Length of stags averages 200cm (6½ft), tail 20cm (8in); height 110cm (3½ft) at the shoulder, hinds are about 10% smaller; stag weight up to 190kg (419lb), hind weight up to 115kg (254lb)

FEATURES
Stags have large, branched antlers. Coat is dark reddish brown in summer with cream underbelly, rump and inner thighs; darker brownish or greyish winter coat. Short tail is a distinctive beige above creamy buff rump patch with no black outline

HABITS
Lives in small herds; stags form sociable groups in spring while regrowing antlers, but become deadly rivals when the rut begins in late September; hinds solitary when giving birth but gather into herds with their offspring and the non-breeding males

FOOD
Plants including grass and leaves; where good grazing/browsing is not available, coarse grasses, heather, dwarf shrubs and other substitutes, which are less nutritious and often result in increased tooth wear; tree bark, especially in winter, when snow covering the ground may also force them to raid farm crops

BREEDING
Rutting late September to end October; births May–June; usually a single calf, but very occasionally twins where food supply is good

YOUNG
Rufous coat with white spots, which disappear within a few weeks of birth

DISTRIBUTION
Most of Scotland, including most of the islands, south-west England, Cumbria and parts of East Anglia; small numbers in the New Forest and other parts of southern England; parts of Ireland; commonly kept in deer parks in Scotland and Ireland

present all year round
not present

Where to see red deer

• Deer parks are the best places to see red deer. Even rutting behaviour can be observed, with no risk of causing disturbance to the animals. Deer parks, such as Richmond Park in Surrey and Windsor Park in Berkshire, are often marked on road maps and may be associated with stately homes. Many National Trust properties have deer parks.

• Calves may be seen with their mothers in June and July, especially in deer parks.

• Red deer may be observed in the wild in much of Scotland, especially the Highlands and Islands, on Exmoor (straddling the Devon-Somerset border), the Quantocks (Somerset) and in the New Forest (Hampshire). Wild deer are timid and should not be approached. In forested areas, the animals may be abundant but hard to see.

• Always take care when watching red deer, especially during the rut when you should watch from a distance through binoculars. The deer may attack intruding humans, causing serious injury.

• PROTECTED SPECIES
Red deer are protected during the summer by a closed hunting season. The precise dates are different in Scotland from those that apply in England and Wales.

The red squirrel

NAMES
Common name: red squirrel
Scientific name: *Sciurus vulgaris*

HABITAT
Conifer, especially pine, forests; occasionally deciduous woodland

STATUS
Probably about 160,000 individuals in Britain

SIZE
Length head and body 18–24cm (7–9½in), tail 14–20cm (5½–8in); weight 230–350g (8–12¼oz); males generally larger than females

FEATURES
Dark brown in winter with prominent ear tufts; bright chestnut in summer; some individuals are black

HABITS
Lives in trees, running and leaping from branch to branch; does not hibernate but may remain inactive during bad weather

FOOD
Pine seeds, hazel nuts, beech mast, chestnuts, berries; in spring and summer, buds, tree flowers, bark and insects; may also nibble fungi that grow under tree bark

BREEDING
Young born March–April, sometimes second litter in July–August; usually 3 or 4 but up to 6 in a litter

NEST
Made of twigs usually bitten from trees; leaves still attached to the twigs are visible on the nest, called a drey

YOUNG
Weaned at 8–10 weeks, able to breed at about 9 months

SIGNS
Nibbled pine cone cores; hazel nuts shattered into jagged pieces

DISTRIBUTION
Scattered throughout Scotland and Ireland; parts of East Anglia, Lancashire and Wales, including Anglesey; Isle of Wight and Brownsea Island

☐ present all year round
☐ not present

Where to see red squirrels

• Red squirrels are fairly widespread in wooded parts of Scotland but the easiest places to see them include the National Trust (NT) Red Squirrel Reserve in Formby on the Lancashire coast, and the RSPB reserve at Loch Garten in Scotland, also famed for its ospreys.

• Brownsea Island (NT) has red squirrels and can be visited by hourly boat services from Sandbanks or Poole in Dorset throughout the summer months.

• On the Isle of Wight, red squirrels can be seen in Parkhurst Forest and Firestone Copse (Forestry Commission) and in Walters Copse (NT).

• Scattered populations remain in the Midlands and the Lake District, at Newborough Warren on Anglesey and at Cragside (NT) in Northumberland.

• PROTECTED SPECIES
The red squirrel is listed under Schedules 5 and 6 of the Wildlife and Countryside Act, 1981, which grants it protection from trapping, shooting and all forms of interference. Tampering with its nests is also prohibited, although this protection does not extend to trees in which the red squirrel makes its nests nor prevent felling of woodland where the red squirrel lives.

The roe deer

NAMES
Common name: roe deer
Scientific name: *Capreolus capreolus*

HABITAT
Mainly woodland, including young plantations with plenty of undergrowth; open moorland in Scotland; reedy marshland and occasionally farmland; some suburban areas

STATUS
Around 300,000 individuals in Britain with numbers increasing

SIZE
Height 63–67cm (24½–27in) at the shoulder, head and neck another 30cm (12in); weight adult 18–30kg (39½–66lb); bucks slightly bigger and heavier than does

FEATURES
Coat sandy to reddish brown in summer, greyish brown to blackish in winter; tail inconspicuous, variable pale buff rump patch; black nose and nose band, white chin; short antlers with maximum of three points

HABITS
Normally solitary or in small family groups; mostly nocturnal but often seen out in the daytime browsing for food

FOOD
Shrubs and young trees, including foliage, bark, fruit and nuts, and especially acorns; also feeds on vegetation from a wide range of plants such as grasses, ferns, heathers and brambles; woodland fungi

BREEDING
Rut from July to late August, and kids born in the following year from May to June; single kid or twins, occasionally triplets

YOUNG
Brown with white spots; resemble adults within a few months

DISTRIBUTION
Throughout Scotland, northern England and the Midlands; scattered in the south; absent from Ireland, Isle of Man and Isle of Wight and Wales

■ present all year round
□ not present

Where to see roe deer

• Many forestry plantations have deer observation hides, or 'high seats', up in the trees. Roe deer can also be observed from birdwatchers' hides in wooded areas. The best time to look is at dawn and dusk near recognised feeding areas, because roe deer usually spend the day under cover.

• Roe are common in the New Forest, Hampshire, Thetford Forest on the Norfolk–Suffolk border, Grizedale Forest in the Lake District, Cumbria, and over much of Scotland. For more information contact the local Forestry Commission office, or visit www.forestry.gov.uk

The stoat

NAMES
Common name: stoat
Scientific name: *Mustela erminea*

HABITAT
Moorland, upland, farmland, woodland – anywhere with enough food and cover

STATUS
Estimated to be around 462,000 individuals prior to the breeding season; numbers may be declining

SIZE
Length males 25–45cm (10–18in) from nose to tail, females about 35cm (14in); weight males 200–445g (7–15½oz), females 140–280g (5–10oz)

FEATURES
Chestnut brown above, creamy white or yellowish white underneath; end of tail black

HABITS
Active by day and night; hunts by stalking and pouncing, may wait in ambush, or search for prey; typically active in bursts of 30–40 minutes, then rests for 1–4 hours

FOOD
Rabbits, small mammals and birds. Males often prey on young rabbits and hares plus birds and small rodents, while females may eat mainly voles

BREEDING
Females are sexually mature at 5 weeks; males at 1 year. Mate in spring and summer; implantation delayed for 9–11 months before 3–4 week spring gestation

NEST
Several dens in stone walls, rocky crevices or in nests and burrows of prey; may be lined with rodent fur

YOUNG
One litter a year, 5–12 kits (usually 7–9) born in March or April; eyes open at 4–6 weeks; independent by early autumn

SIGNS
Frequently seen as road casualties; droppings black with a musky smell when fresh, but hard to find

DISTRIBUTION
Sparsely distributed throughout most of Britain and Ireland, Outer Hebrides and other, smaller islands, but not Orkney

■ present all year round
□ not present

Where to see stoats

• Moorland, grassland and woodland all over Britain and Ireland may support stoats. Look for areas that are likely to have plenty of food and cover, such as rough grassland, rabbit warrens and scrub. Stone walls and hedgerows can prove fruitful sites for stoat spotting because stoats frequently forage along them, looking for small mammals.

• The grounds of Mount Grace Priory, near Northallerton in North Yorkshire, are teeming with rabbits and the resident stoats have become TV celebrities, featuring in the BBC documentary *The Life of Mammals*. They can be seen popping up out of the ancient water ducts and, unusually for stoats, are not shy of spectators.

• The dry stone walls of the Yorkshire and Durham Dales and the rough grassland and low-lying meadows of the Somerset Levels are all stoat strongholds. East Anglian game estates are also good spots for stoats. Try the nature reserve at Holkham or the woods near Thetford.

• Unfortunately, stoats are among the more frequent victims of road traffic. Dashing out from the verge or hedge to cross the road, they are often hit by cars, which are among the few things that travel faster than they do.

The water shrew

NAMES
Common name: water shrew
Scientific name: *Neomys fodiens*

HABITAT
Streams and ponds, especially clear waters; woodlands and hedges, occasionally some distance from water; reported among boulders on Scottish beaches

STATUS
Estimated 1,900,000 individuals; least common of British mainland shrews

SIZE
Length 6.5–9.5cm (2½–3¾in), tail 4.5–7.5cm (1¾–3in); weight 12–18g (¼–¾oz), but pregnant female about 10g (⅓oz) heavier

FEATURES
Velvety black fur above, and white, grey or yellowish below; small ears, often white tipped; tiny eyes; fringe of stiff hairs along underside of tail and also edging hind toes; small, red-tipped teeth

HABITS
Active, scurries around in dense grass and lush, low vegetation; swims well and often; solitary except when mother is rearing young

FOOD
Large quantities of freshwater shrimps, aquatic insect larvae, small snails; also insects, worms and other invertebrates; occasionally small fish and young frogs

BREEDING
Some females have first litter when 2–3 months old, but most breed in summer following birth; mating occurs April–June; usually 2 or 3 litters born per year, each with an average of 6 young

NEST
Underground in tunnel system or beneath a log; woven from dry grass

YOUNG
Born after 14–21 days gestation; leave nest at about 6 weeks old; young less distinctively marked than adult; fur brown above and dingy buff beneath

DISTRIBUTION
Patchy, but found throughout mainland Britain and also on some offshore islands

present all year round

not present

Where to see water shrews

• Water shrews are lone creatures, and you are unlikely to see one by accident. A good place to look is alongside a small chalk stream. Talk to local fishermen first as they may be able to direct you to the best place to sit and wait.

• Watercress beds are a favourite habitat of water shrews. Always ask before entering private land. The owner of the cress bed may well be able to confirm whether or not you are likely to see water shrews. You will need to be patient and sit quietly.

• Dawn and dusk are the best times to search, as water shrews are not usually active during the day.

• PROTECTED SPECIES
All shrews have a limited degree of protection under the Wildlife and Countryside Act, 1981. You are not allowed to trap water shrews without a licence.

The water vole

NAMES
Common name: water vole
Scientific name: *Arvicola terrestris*

HABITAT
Beside lowland rivers, streams and ponds, often passes undetected in reedbeds; sometimes found in uplands, along urban rivers and on salt marshes

STATUS
Population estimated at about 1.2 million; common in a few scattered areas; had declined to 875,000 by 1998

SIZE
Length head and body 14–22cm (5½–9in), tail 9–14cm (3½–5½in); weight 150–300g (5½–10½oz)

FEATURES
Chestnut brown silky fur, rounded face, snub nose, very small ears and thin dark tail; sexes similar

HABITS
Shy but often active in daylight as well as at night; swims in still or slow-flowing water; emerges to sit on haunches and nibble food held between paws

FOOD
Wide range of plants especially grasses and sedges but also roots and bulbs and occasionally small animals such as fish

BREEDING
Litter size generally 5; usually 3–4 litters per year, born March–October

NEST
By the waterside, a burrow chamber or ball-shaped nest woven from stems of reeds, rushes or grasses. Built among dense tussocks where water table is high

YOUNG
Fur darker, greyer and less glossy than adult's coat; weaned at 3 weeks

SIGNS
Small groups of shiny, greenish, cylindrical droppings in latrines – areas of close-cropped grass, sometimes with small heaps of cropped vegetation; tiny star-shaped footprints in mud

DISTRIBUTION
Most of southern and central England, eastern and lowland Scotland, parts of Wales; also on the Isle of Wight and Anglesey, absent from the Isle of Man and Ireland

present all year round

not present

Where to see water voles

• Water voles are more often heard than seen, as they scuffle in the vegetation and plop into the water. Search slow rivers and reedy ponds, and choose a mild day as water voles tend not to come out in extremes of heat or cold.

• Water vole tracks can be seen in the smooth mud where they enter and leave the water. Look for runs and tunnels in dense waterside vegetation. Feeding signs include small patches of cropped grasses, sedges and reeds, with little piles of discarded vegetable matter.

• Tame water voles can often be seen in the duck pens at Wildfowl and Wetland Trust sites, such as Slimbridge, Martin Mere and the London Wetland Centre in Barnes, south-west London. There is also a healthy population in the Norfolk Broads. Surprisingly, an increasingly good place to see water voles is in cities and towns located on rivers where the species has been encouraged or reintroduced.

• PROTECTED SPECIES
By 1998 water vole numbers had declined so much that the Wildlife and Countryside Act was revised to give them some legal protection. Although it is not illegal to trap and kill water voles, their burrows are now protected and they must not be disturbed in their homes. This means that river managers in particular are obliged by law to take account of this small mammal. They cannot, for example, permit waterside engineering works that might destroy water vole habitats and burrows through the use of heavy machinery.

The weasel

NAMES
Common name: weasel,
mouse hunter, cane
Scientific name: *Mustela nivalis*

HABITAT
Mainly grassland, farmland and
woodland; especially rough, grassy
patches with high vole populations

STATUS
Approximately 450,000 individuals
before breeding season; several million
after successful season

SIZE
Length nose to tail, males average 21cm
(8¼in), females 18cm (7in); weight,
males 120g (4¼oz), females 65g (2¼oz)

FEATURES
Long, slim body, fur russet brown on
back, underparts white with small brown
patches on throat; tail shortish; fur stays
brown in winter in British populations

HABITS
Active day and night; hunts by smell and
detecting movement; short bouts of
activity are interspersed with longer rest
periods in den

FOOD
Small rodents, especially field voles, but
also shrews and rats; also young rabbits,
squirrels, small birds and eggs

BREEDING
Mates throughout spring and summer;
gestation 5 weeks; litters may be born
until late August; 1 sometimes 2 litters
per year; 4–9 young per litter, usually 4–6

NEST
Den sited in collapsed stone walls,
among tree roots or in grassland under
rocks or corrugated iron sheets

YOUNG
Born naked and blind, eyes open at 4
weeks, kill own prey at 8 weeks, leave
nest at 9–12 weeks

SIGNS
Droppings 3–6cm (1¼–2½in) long,
twisted, dark, full of hair, feathers and
pieces of bone; easily overlooked

DISTRIBUTION
Throughout mainland Britain and some
large islands, including Skye, Isle of
Wight and Anglesey; absent from
Ireland, Channel Islands, Isle of Man
and smaller islands

present all year round
not present

Where to see weasels

• Weasels are elusive and, because they are so small, spotting them is difficult. Try seeking out places where they forage regularly. Wait alongside the grassy edges of stone walls and hedgerows where they chase their prey. Weasels may even pop out of their dens in stone walls and log piles to keep an eye on a human. If a weasel dashes past once, wait a while, keep still and quiet, and it will probably be back again shortly to investigate or continue hunting.

• Field voles are prolific in rough grassland so such areas are ideal for finding weasels. Watch for voles fleeing from weasels, scattering to avoid being cornered. A weasel may even show itself because all of its concentration is on the hunt. Farmland, wet meadows and young plantations are also often rich in voles, and therefore home to weasels. Estates with farm woodland schemes or rough ground left for game birds are good places to look.

• On a larger scale, the conifer plantations found in the uplands of Britain, such as Kielder Forest in Northumberland, have places that are ideal for weasels in the tussocky rides and firebreaks between the dense stands of trees. Closer to towns, patches of rough or abandoned ground may house weasels. The sight of owls or kestrels foraging is always a good sign, because it indicates that there is plenty of small mammal prey available for predators to feed on.

The wild goat

NAMES
Common name: wild goat, feral goat
Scientific name: *Capra hircus*

HABITAT
Rocky mountainsides and steep slopes; open moorland and grassland; may move below 500m (1640ft) in harsh weather

STATUS
Total population around 3500

SIZE
Height 60–70cm (2–2ft 4in) at shoulder; length 120–130cm (3ft 9in–4ft 4in); tail 10–12cm (4–5in); weight 25–65kg (55–145lb); males larger than females

FEATURES
Thick, hairy fur variably coloured; ears point directly upwards; both sexes have horns

HABITS
Wary, active at night and during the day; lives in small herds

FOOD
Almost any edible plant material, including leaves, grass and bark

BREEDING
Rut (mating season) in autumn; gestation period about 150 days. One or occasionally two kids born January–April (mainly March)

YOUNG
Kids stay with mother for up to six months before becoming fully independent; often remain with same herd

SIGNS
Droppings and footprints similar to those of sheep, but wild goat's toe prints splay out more at the tips

DISTRIBUTION
Scattered localities mostly in Scotland (two-thirds of population) but also along the England-Scotland border, in North Wales and a few places in south-west England; also on some islands

■ present all year round
□ not present

Where to see wild goats

• In Scotland, along the eastern side of Loch Lomond, goats live near Inversnaid Lodge and can be seen from the West Highland Way. Farther north, they may be seen on the north side of Loch Morar, near Newtonmore on the A9 and also in the Findhorn Valley. Some goats live on the Mull of Kintyre and on several Scottish islands, including the Isle of Rhum National Nature Reserve. A wild goat park is situated between Newton Stewart and New Galloway on the A712.

• In England, wild goats can be seen at Brean Down in Somerset, at the Valley of the Rocks in north Devon, and on Lundy in the Bristol Channel. They also live in College Valley in Northumbria on Newton Tors.

• Wild goats live near the Llanberis Pass in Snowdonia in North Wales and are especially easy to see around the slate quarries of the Padarn Country Park. They also live at Cwm Bychan.

• The best sites to see wild goats in Ireland are the Wicklow Mountains, just 10km (6 miles) south of Dublin, and the Burren in County Clare.

The wood mouse

NAMES
Common name: wood mouse,
long-tailed field mouse
Scientific name: *Apodemus sylvaticus*

HABITAT
Woodland, hedgerows, parks, gardens,
farmland, sand dunes and mountainsides

STATUS
Estimated 38,500,000 individuals,
although population fluctuates.

SIZE
Length 8–10cm (3⅛–4in), tail
7.5–10cm (3–4in); ears 15mm (⅝in);
weight 13–27g (½–1oz)

FEATURES
Dark brown fur above, often with a
sandy or reddish tinge, and paler brown
or yellowish fur along the flanks; whitish
fur below, often with a yellow chest spot
of variable size that is always separated
from the brown upper fur by whitish fur

HABITS
Mainly nocturnal; usually active on the
ground, but may climb into trees and
bushes to feed or nest

FOOD
Seeds, grain, fruits, green plants;
invertebrates, including worms

BREEDING
Up to 9 (usually 4–7) young per litter,
several litters per year, typically
March–October

NEST
Usually underground in burrow system,
or below logs or among roots; may use
holes in trees or buildings or nestboxes;
lines nest with dead leaves, moss and
grass

YOUNG
Fur greyer than adult on back and
underside, no yellow spot or streak on
chest

SIGNS
Hard to detect, but hazel nuts are
gnawed in a characteristic way, leaving
roundish holes with tooth marks on
outer shell; tooth marks may also
traverse opened edge of nut

DISTRIBUTION
All of mainland Britain, Ireland and most
offshore islands

present all year round
not present

Where to see wood mice

• Waiting quietly in woodland at night
is one way to see wood mice, but they
are wary creatures and difficult to spot.
Use a torch covered with red paper –
red light will not disturb them, but
white light will keep them away – and
never go to isolated places alone.

• Alternatively, attract them into the
garden by putting out bird seed and
grain, preferably on tables specifically
designed for the purpose. For advice,
contact the Mammal Society at 2B
Inworth Street, London SW11 3EP
(telephone 020 7350 2200) or visit
www.abdn.ac.uk/mammal

Executive Editor	Nick Rowe
Editor	Marion Paull
Editorial Assistant	Jo Whitford
Art Editor	Phil Gibbs
Production	Teresa Wellborne
Publishing Manager	Nina Hathway

This book was designed, edited and produced by Eaglemoss Publications Ltd, using material first published in the partwork *Wildlife of Britain* and subsequently in the Reader's Digest *Wildlife Watch* series.

Copyright © Eaglemoss Publications Ltd/Midsummer Books Ltd 2008

Published by
Eaglemoss Consumer Publications Ltd,
Electra House, Electra Way,
Crewe, Cheshire CW1 6WZ
Telephone 01270 270 050
Website www.dairydiary.co.uk

ISBN 13: 978-0-9554232-5-3

Printed in China by Leo Paper Products Ltd

10 9 8 7 6 5 4 3 2 1

CREDITS

Photographs: Front cover NP/Owen Newman; 3 NP/Owen Newman; 4(tl) NHPA/Stephen Dalton, (clu) NPL/TJ Rich, (cl) NHPA/Andy Rouse, (blu) NHPA/Manfred Danegger, (bl) OSF/Mike Powells; 6(tr) NPL/Gary K Smith, (bl) Ardea/Jim Zipp; 7(tr) NHPA/Alan Williams, (br) FLPA/Derek Middleton; 8-9 FLPA/David Hosking; 10(b) BC/Bob Glover; 11(t) BC/WS Paton; 12 BC; 13 BC; 14 FLPA/F Merlet; 15 FLPA/Chris Newton; 16 NP/Owen Newman; 18 BC/Jane Burton; 19(t) OSF, (b) Ardea/JB & S Bottomley; 20(t) NHPA/R Hosking; 21(t) NHPA/M Leach, (b)FLPA/R Tidman; 22(b) Alamy/Andrew Darrington; 23 NHPA/Manfred Danegger; 24 NHPA/Manfred Danegger; 25 FLPA/Silvestris; 26 FLPA/Silvestris; 27 BC/R Maier; 28 NV/Jason Venus; 29 BC/R Maier; 30 Laurie Campbell; 31 FLPA/D Middleton; 32 Aquila/M Birkenhead; 33 Aquila/M&V Lane; 35 Ardea/J Mason; 36 FLPA/E&D Hosking; 37 BC; 38 Woodfall/S Austin; 39 NV/Heather Angel; 40 FLPA/E Hosking; 42 NPL/D Nill; 44 NPL/Xi Zhi Nong; 45 Aquila/D Luck; 46 OSF/R Redfern; 47 BC/Kim Taylor; 48 BC/Colin Varndell; 49 Aquila; 50 NPL/Jim Hallett; 51 Ardea/Pat Morris; 52-53 FLPA/Mike Lane; 54 FLPA/M Withers; 55(tl) OSF/R Redfern, (cr) Mike Read; 56 OSF/Mark Hamblin; 57(tr) FLPA/M Withers, (b) FLPA/F Merlet; 58 FLPA/M Withers; 59 OSF/Richard Packwood; 60 FLPA/R Bender; 61 NHPA/Manfred Danegger; 62 Andy Rouse; 63 NHPA/Manfred Danegger; 64 BC; 65 David Tipling; 66 David Tipling; 67 NPL/George McCarthy; 68 NP; 69 NP; 70 BC/Jane Burton; 71 NP/Owen Newman; 72 NP/Owen Newman; 73 NP/Owen Newman; 74 FLPA/R Tidman; 75 Ardea/Ian Beames; 76 OSF/Harold Taylor; 77 FLPA/Robert Canis; 78 FLPA/Silvestris; 79 FLPA/Roger Wilmhurst; 80 NPL/A Harrington; 82 Aquila/JF Preedy; 83 OSF/M Leach; 84 BC/George McCarthy; 85 FLPA/E&D Hosking; 86 NPL/A Coope; 87 FLPA/OW Grewcock; 88 FLPA/HD Brandl; 89 FLPA/Silvestris; 90 FLPA/F Merlet; 91 FLPA/E&D Hosking; 92 BC/Kim Taylor; 93 BC/Jane Burton; 94 BC/Kim Taylor; 95-96 NPL/Elio della Ferrera; 98 Ardea/Ian Beames; 99 FLPA; 100 Mike Read; 101 FLPA/RP Lawrence; 102 Still Pictures/John Cancalosi; 103 Mike Read; 104-106 Neil McIntyre; 107 Mike Read; 108 OSF/K Ringland; 109 Mike Read; 110 FLPA/T Hamblin; 111 RSPCA/K&P Wolf; 112 RSPCA/N Rolstone; 113 FLPA/C Newton; 114 Ardea/JP Ferrero; 115 FLPA/Silvestris; 116 BC/C Cardwell; 117 Aquila/JF Preedy; 118 NPL/T Mangelson; 119 OSF/L&T Bomford; 120 BC/Hans Reinhard; 121 NHPA/R Tidman; 122 Neil McIntyre; 123 Trip/Van Greaves; 124 Laurie Campbell; 125 OSF/N Benvie; 126 NHPA/Manfred Danegger; 128 FLPA/R Maier; 129 NHPA/Manfred Danegger; 130 NPL/D Nill; 131 NHPA/William Paton; 132-133 NPL/Andrew Parkinson; 134 Mike Read; 135 NHPA/Laurie Campbell; 136 NV/Jason Venus; 137 FLPA/W Rohdich; 138 BC/Gordon Langsbury; 139 FLPA/W Rohdich; 140 OSF/GA Maclean; 141 NV/Heather Angel; 142 BC/J Markham; 144(tr) OSF/GA Maclean, (cr) NV/Heather Angel; 145 Ardea/Ian Beames; 146 FLPA/S Malowski; 147 BC/Jane Burton; 148 Andy Rouse; 149 Andy Rouse; 150 BC; 151 Andy Rouse; 152 OSF/D Boag; 153 NHPA/Stephen Dalton; 154 OSF/PK Sharpe; 155 OSF/T Shephard; 156 OSF/T Shephard; 157 BC/Jane Burton; 158 BC/A Potts; 159 BC/R Jordan; 160(t) NP/EA Janes, (b) BC/C&S Hood; 161 Sealphotos; 162-163 NPL/John Cancalosi; 164 NP; 165 NP/EA Janes; 166 NP/Owen Newman; 167 FLPA/E&D Hosking; 168 FLPA/R Tidman; 169 P Chippendale; 170 BC/Colin Varndell; 171 BC/C&S Hood; 172 BC; 173 David Tipling; 174 Ardea/JP Ferrero; 175 BC; 176 BC; 177 Neil McIntyre; 178 Kit Houghton; 179 NP/Hugh Miles; 180 NHPA/M Danegger; 181 BC/Kim Taylor; 182 BC; 183 Pat Morris; 184 Mike Read; 185 Aquila/R Seigal; 186 NHPA/M Leach; 187 OSF/T Shephard; 188 NP/P Sterry; 189 OSF/R Redfern; 190 Neil McIntyre; 191 Aquila/J de Meester.

All illustrations by John Ridyard

Key to photo library abbreviations: BC = Bruce Coleman Ltd, FLPA = Frank Lane Photo Agency, NHPA = Natural History Photo Agency, NP = Nature Photographers, NPL = Nature Picture Library, NV = Heather Angel/Natural Visions, OSF = Oxford Scientific Films.